Chalk It Up!

Written by Cary Seeman and Taree Bollinger
Illustrated by Bev Armstrong

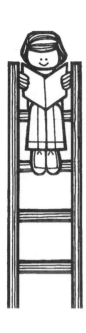

The Learning Works

Illustrations by Bev Armstrong

Cover Production by Melissa Marie Johns

Typesetting and Editorial Production by Clark Editorial & Design

Special thanks to our Chalk It Up! *cover kids: Daniel Dockendorf, Brittany Alyssa Nichols, and Faryn Richardson*

Copyright©1997
The Learning Works, Inc.
P.O. Box 6187
Santa Barbara, California 93160

ISBN: 0-88160-276-0

Introduction

Pippi Longstocking wasn't one to be confined by the boundaries of paper. When she drew her horse, Pippi demonstrated something all children know without being taught: A horse simply will not fit on an 8.5" x 11" sheet of paper.

> "But Pippi," said the teacher impatiently, "why in the world aren't you drawing on your paper?"
>
> "I filled that long ago. There isn't room enough for my whole horse on that little snip of a paper," said Pippi. "Just now I'm working on his front legs, but when I get to his tail I guess I'll have to go out in the hall."
>
> (*Pippi Longstocking*, Astrid Lindgren, Viking Press, New York, 1950, p. 56)

Why restrict students by the size of art paper or even to the space within the four walls of the classroom? Grab a box of chalk and head outdoors! On the following pages of *Chalk It Up!*, you'll learn how to take advantage of your school playground or sidewalk.

Chalk opens up whole new worlds and offers new perspectives where students can literally "get into" their lesson. There's a lot more learning taking place when students draw and stand within the chalk outlines of Columbus' ships than if they simply read about the measurements in a book. Dinosaurs become incredibly more massive and imposing when one is standing next to a life-sized chalk drawing. And it's so much easier to visualize just how big Texas is when it's drawn to scale next to Rhode Island.

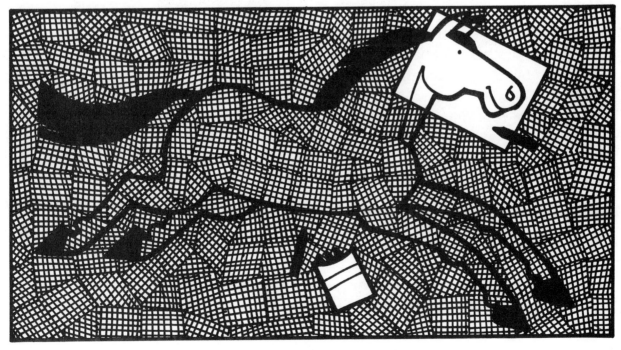

3

Contents

Getting Started

A Chalk Curriculum

Social Studies

Science

Language Arts

Contents

Chalk Games to Play

Chalk Is Cheap

Why chalk? Its creative power is endless, and besides, it's inexpensive. A piece of chalk has many things stored in it when a child's imagination takes hold. Chalk projects are also perfect for school playgrounds. You can use and reuse the same surfaces and then wait for the rain to wash it away or little feet to wear it off. It fits all school budgets. To help make it even more affordable, a recipe is included that students can use to make sidewalk chalk as a class project (see page 7).

Something for Everyone

Chalk It Up! includes group activities as well as individual projects. All exercises use creative thinking, cooperative learning, and decision-making skills. The novelty of these activities gives added relevance to subjects such as math, geography, language arts, and social studies.

This book is divided into three easy-to-follow sections. "Getting Started" includes suggestions on playground etiquette, special techniques for working with chalk, and quick and easy warm-up exercises to get students accustomed to the freedom of working outdoors.

Each lesson in "A Chalk Curriculum" includes a description of the activity, a list of supplies, preparation instructions, step-by-step directions, follow-up discussion starters, and extenders to increase the difficulty of the lesson for gifted and highly talented students. Some lessons also include additional suggestions for applying the same lesson plan to other subjects. The major curriculum areas covered in each lesson are identified for your convenience. They are located in the upper corner of each page.

Part three, "Chalk Games to Play," includes the rules for popular children's playground games that are played on a hard surface within a chalk diagram. These games offer another opportunity to incorporate deductive reasoning, problem solving, and visualization exercises into your daily plans while experiencing the freedom of an expanded classroom.

Grab your chalk and let's get drawing!

Making Sidewalk Chalk

This simple, nontoxic sidewalk chalk can be made in the classroom in one simple lesson. Allow 30 minutes preparation time and two to three hours for hardening. This recipe makes two or three very large chalk sticks.

What You Need

- one cup water
- up to 1/4 cup liquid tempera paint
- two squirts of dish soap
- one capful of vinegar
- two cups plaster of Paris
- one empty toilet paper tube per chalk stick
- petroleum jelly
- tongue depressors (optional)
- masking tape
- disposable "mixing bowls" (coffee cans, microwave dinner bowls, etc.)

What You Do

1. Seal off one end of the toilet paper tube with masking tape.

2. Rub petroleum jelly on the inside of each toilet paper tube. Optional: Use tongue depressors to spread the petroleum jelly. Don't overdo it; the purpose of the petroleum jelly is to keep the plaster of Paris from sticking to the tube.

3. Mix the water, vinegar, dish soap, and plaster of Paris in a disposable mixing bowl. (You may need to adjust the amounts slightly to get the right texture.)

4. Add the tempera paint and blend to the desired color. Paint can be swirled into the plaster of Paris for a special effect.

5. Pour the mixture into the toilet paper tube. When the plaster is hard, peel away the toilet paper tube.

You may wish to divide the class into small work groups. Each group can make one color of chalk. The chalk sticks can then be divided into sets.

Behavior Guidelines

Before you venture outdoors, discuss rules for behavior with your students. It is a good idea to be aware of and to anticipate potential problems before you begin the activities.

1. Set up a meeting place on the playground where students assemble to begin lessons.

2. Have each student place a library book in a special box and place the box along a "reading wall." If students or groups complete the activity before the rest of the class, they can go directly to the designated area, find their book, and sit and read.

3. Alert the students to a whistle signal. If the class gets too loud or additional instructions need to be given, blow your whistle. Students should stop what they are doing, sit down, and wait for your instructions. If the class is spread out over a large area, the whistle becomes a signal to return to the original meeting place.

4. If a student breaks a rule, he or she should be sent to a "time-out chair" for a designated period of time. The chair should be placed within the viewing distance of the teacher.

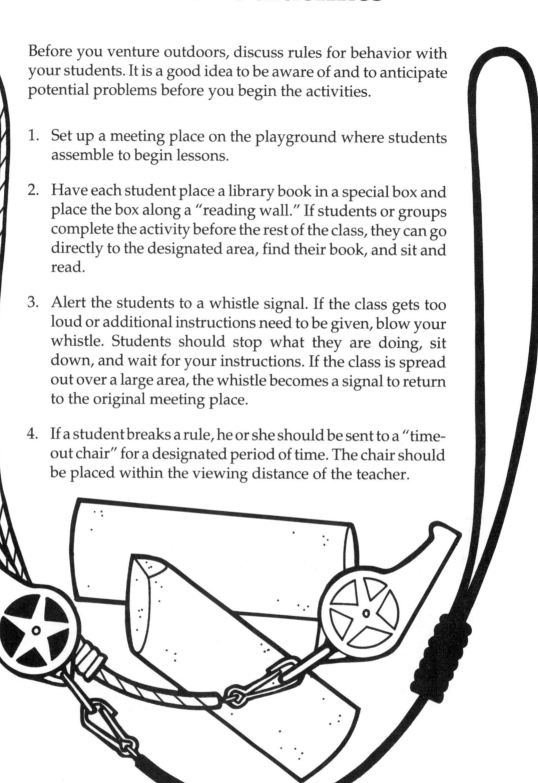

Behavior Guidelines

5. Let the class brainstorm rules about using the bathroom, getting drinks, talking to other groups, and so forth. When students have a voice in the rule-making process, they tend to follow the rules better.

6. Be mindful of other classes when working on the playground. Other teachers will be more supportive of your efforts if you control the noise and make sure groups do not work within close viewing distance of another class.

7. Use parent volunteers. If the class is divided into groups working in separate areas of the playground, send a parent along with each group. This will conserve your energy and eliminate the need for you to run continuously from group to group.

8. Identify areas and items that are off-limits; for example, no running through the work areas, no playing on the monkey bars, no leaving the blacktop, and so forth.

9

Helpful Hints

Make Tags to Identify Team Members

Many of the lessons and games in *Chalk It Up!* require the students to be identified as a team or group member. The students can make identification badges by cutting out various shapes from different colors of construction paper. Students can also adhere stickers to plastic name tag holders to differentiate team members. Incorporate the tags into the activity by having the students produce their own designs on plain paper using computer clip art.

Have students pin the tags to their shirts or jackets with members of the same team displaying identical badges. Depending on the nature of the activity, pinning the extra tags on the students' backs or arms may increase visibility from all directions.

Drawing Circles With Chalk

Drawing chalk circles on the playground for various games and activities can be simplified by following these steps:

1. Cut a piece of string the length of the radius of your circle.

2. Tie one end of the string to your piece of chalk. Tie a knot at the other end and insert a tack.

3. Tape a piece of cardboard to the center of the area where the circle is to be drawn.

4. Have a student stand on the edge of the cardboard.

5. Insert the tack into the cardboard. Extend the string to its full length and draw the circle.

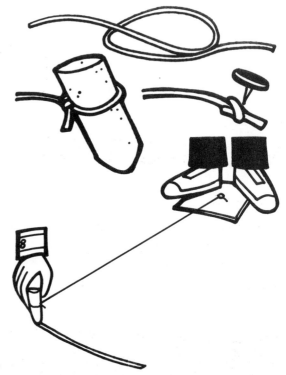

You might want to have the students work in pairs with one student holding the cardboard and the tack in place so that they don't come loose while the circle is being drawn.

Helpful Hints

Using Chalk Powder to Draw Straight Lines

By borrowing from the technique of drawing wallpapering plumb lines, anyone can draw straight lines on the playground.

1. Dip a string of desired length in powdered chalk until it is fully coated. Note: To make powdered chalk, save small unusable bits of chalk. Place them in a coffee can and grind them into a fine dust.

2. Stretch the string tight against the ground. One student holds each end, pulling the string taut.

3. A third student gives the string a flick (snaps the string). The powder will transfer to the cement or blacktop surface. If the string is fairly long, flick it in several spots.

Carpet Pieces to Protect Knees

To protect knees when working on hard surfaces, have each student bring in a small piece of carpet. Ask your local carpet dealer to donate carpet samples for this purpose. Size and color can vary. Bicycle/skateboard knee pads or gardening knee pads can also be used. Knee pads work best for projects when the students are moving from place to place and getting up and down a lot.

11

Helpful Hints

Make a Marker #1

Making markers to use as game pieces is as easy as folding a flag. Start with an 8.5" x 11" sheet of copy paper or notebook paper. (Construction paper is too heavy.)

1. Fold it in half lengthwise.

2. Make a second lengthwise fold.

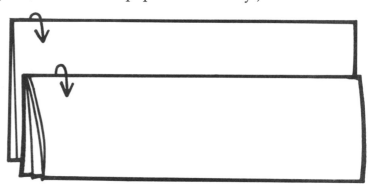

3. Fold one end up diagonally, forming a triangle.

4. Fold the triangle to the left and then fold it down diagonally.

5. Continue folding up, left, down, left, until you can no longer make another fold.

6. Tuck the remaining paper into the open end of the triangle.

7. Each child can color or decorate his or her marker to make it unique.

Helpful Hints

Make a Marker #2

Another type of marker can be made by folding the same size paper as follows:

1. Fold paper in half, lengthwise, two times.

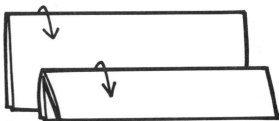

2. Fold one tip up diagonally and the other down.

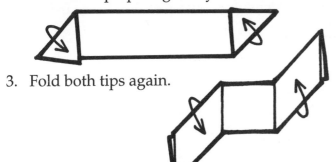

3. Fold both tips again.

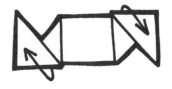

4. Fold the tips back down over the previous fold.

5. Flip the marker over and fold one side halfway up the back.

6. Wrap the other side over the side you just folded and tuck in the ends. Press the finished markers in books and place the book under a chair for maximum flattening.

7. Students can use the marker as is or they can gently pull apart the sections to make three-dimensional shapes. In some cases, a carefully positioned piece of tape may prove advantageous.

Helpful Hints

Making Dice

You can create your own set of dice by gluing numbers to the sides of large blocks of foam or by covering the sides of a square-shaped tissue box. You can also construct cubes using the pattern shown below.

Cube Pattern for Dice

To make a cube, trace the pattern below onto lightweight cardboard or tagboard. Cut it out. Color each side a different color or add numbers or words. Fold in the same direction along all dotted lines. Glue or tape flaps to sides. For larger cubes, enlarge this pattern using an overhead projector.

Chalk Warm-Ups

Let your students warm up to the freedom of working in an open-air environment by delving into some of the activities in this section. These ideas will give you and your students a chance to try new and motivating ways to review, practice, or expand objectives from your regular lesson plans. All of the activities can be done in just a few minutes and require little or no extra planning or materials (except for sidewalk chalk, of course!).

Language Arts

- Take a practice spelling test. It's a lot more fun doing repetitive drills on the playground than sitting at your desk.

- Scramble the week's spelling words and hand each student a copy of the list. Let the students unscramble them. The playground offers lots of space for trial and error. Students can circle their final answer.

Mathematics

- Have students work in pairs. Give each pair a cup with an assortment of objects (6 paper clips, 10 rubber bands, 3 pencils, etc.). The contents of all of the cups should be identical. Ask the pairs to use their chalk to draw a bar graph depicting the objects. As a class, proof the graphs for accuracy and practice reading the graphs. As a special treat or as a holiday activity, give the students an assortment of edibles to graph (pretzels, carrots, raisins, peanuts, etc.). Let the students eat their "data" after they proof their graphs.

Chalk Warm-Ups

Mathematics (continued)

- Practice fractions by having students draw a series of circles. (See page 10 for instructions on how to draw a circle on the playground.) When you state a fraction out loud, the students shade in the correct portion (three-fourths, seven-eighths, two-thirds, etc.) and write the fraction in symbolic form. Note: If the students draw spokes in their circles, shading will be quicker.

- Give the students a list showing pairs of numbers. Have them find the "greatest common factor" (also referred to as the greatest common divisor). Students should first list the factors for each number, then list the common factors (CF), and finally, choose the greatest of the common factors (GCF).

    Example: **16 and 20**
    16   = 1, 2, 4, 8, 16
    20   = 1, 2, 4, 5, 10, 20
    CF   = 1, 2, 4
    GCF = 4

- Ask students to write three- and four-digit multiplication and division problems on the playground in chalk. Have them write the problems using large print. Students can solve each problem as a class or in teams.

Chalk Warm-Ups

Science

- Draw a map of the solar system on the playground. Have the students stand on the planets and "orbit" the sun. Explain that all planets orbit the sun in the same direction. Point out that when the students walk at the same speed, it takes longer for the planets on the outer rings to complete their orbits. Explain that only Pluto's orbit is tilted. All the others lie in a flat plane.

- Reproduce each of the planets using a scale of 4,000 kilometers diameter = 1 foot. Give the students a copy of the chart below or ask them to do the conversion using a calculator. Draw the planets to scale. When you use a larger scale than those normally seen in books, it becomes apparent how much larger Jupiter and Saturn are than Earth. Note: If playground space is limited, draw the planets in concentric circles.

Planet	Diameter in kilometers	Conversion 1 ft. = 4,000 km	Radius	Time to Rotate Sun
Mercury	4,800	1 ft. 2 in.	7 in.	88 days
Venus	12,100	3 ft.	18 in.	225 days
Earth	12,756	3 ft. 2 in.	19 in.	365 days
Mars	6,787	1 ft. 8 in.	10 in.	687 days
Jupiter	142,800	35 ft. 8 in.	17 ft. 10 in.	12 years
Saturn	120,600	30 ft. 2 in.	15 ft. 1 in.	29.5 years
Uranus	51,300	12 ft. 9 in.	6 ft. 4.5 in.	84 years
Neptune	49,100	12 ft. 4 in.	6 ft. 2 in.	165 years
Pluto	2,300	7 in.	3.5 in.	248 years

Chalk It Up!
© The Learning Works, Inc.

Chalk Warm-Ups

Fine Arts and More

- Draw a long line on the playground. Have each student draw one half of a face, piece of fruit, or any other symmetrical object on one side of the line. Students change places and finish one another's drawings.

- Experiment with freehand drawing. Give the students different colors. Let them see what happens when you blend colors. Bind two or three small pieces of blackboard chalk together with a rubber band and create pictures.

- Draw oversized music staffs and use quarter notes, half notes, and whole notes. Have students hop from note to note, staying on each note for the correct count. Include bar lines and have the class try different tempos (2/4, 3/4, 4/4).

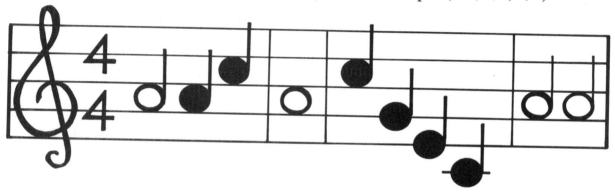

- Practice making patchwork quilt patterns on the playground.

- Improve listening skills by having the students draw from oral instructions. Students should draw a 3 x 3 square grid on the playground. Tell the class that you will only give the instructions once. Ask the students to draw certain items in certain squares.

- Have students make simple dot-to-dot designs on the playground. Then ask them to trade places and fill in one another's drawings.

Setting Sail With Columbus

Objective

Students will use the dimensions of Christopher Columbus' three ships to make full-sized chalk replicas on the playground.

What You Need

- sidewalk chalk
- assorted measuring devices (string, rulers, yardsticks, etc.)
- drawing of Columbus' ships (see page 21)

Before You Begin

As a class, read about Christopher Columbus' voyage to the New World.

Discuss different ways of measuring a large area: yardstick by yardstick, ruler by ruler, measuring a piece of string or ribbon and then stretching it out, measuring a person's foot and then walking off the dimensions, etc.

What You Do

1. Divide the class into three groups. Assign each group to work on one of Columbus' ships: the Niña, the Pinta, or the Santa Maria.

2. Give each group several pieces of chalk and a copy of page 21.

3. Go out to the playground and assign each group of students to a separate work area.

4. Each group should choose a measurement method and make a full-sized chalk outline of its assigned ship.

5. As a class, walk from ship to ship. Have students represent the crew members and stand within the confines of each ship. (The number of crew members is listed on page 21.) If there are fewer students than crew members, have some students represent two crew members by standing with one arm extended to the side. If there are extra students, some can represent supplies and provisions. They should board first and squat in place.

Setting Sail With Columbus

Things to Think About

Discuss how crowded the ships were. Have students consider what it must have been like to live on a ship for more than a month. What discomforts did the sailors have to endure? Ask the students what personal possessions they would take if they were going on a long trip and space was restricted.

Have students share their personal boating experiences and compare the size of Columbus' ships to present-day pleasure crafts.

Talk about the different measuring methods used by the students. Which ones were the most efficient? Why or why not? Which ones were more accurate?

Challenge

Enhance the difficulty of this activity by having the students suggest their own measuring tools. Ask each group to devise an original method of measuring.

More Ways to Play

Make full-sized chalk diagrams of Native American dwellings. Discuss how the dwellings differed. What geographic, climatic, and other factors led them to choose a particular type of dwelling?

Setting Sail With Columbus

Columbus' Ships

Reproduce the outline of the Santa Maria, the Pinta, and the Niña on the playground. Use the appropriate length and width measurements shown below for each ship. Include interior details at your option.

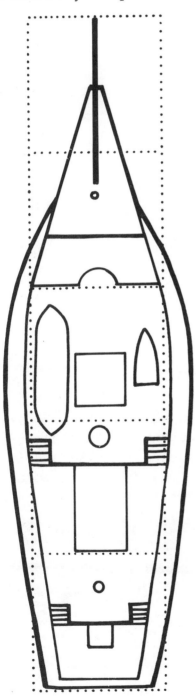

Santa Maria

The Santa Maria was a *carrack*. It probably measured 80 feet in length and 25 feet at the beam (widest point). Forty crewmen set sail on the Santa Maria.

Pinta

The Pinta was a *caravel*. It measured approximately 75 feet in length and 24 feet at the beam. It had a crew of 26.

Niña

The Niña was a caravel like the Pinta, but slightly smaller. It measured 70 feet by 23 feet. The crew numbered 24.

Note: Accurate records of Columbus' ships were never kept. Scholars have based size and configuration estimates on merchant ships of the time. The interior of the two caravels (the Niña and the Pinta) differed slightly in design from the carrack (the Santa Maria). For example, the Santa Maria carried both a long boat and a ship's boat. The Niña and the Pinta only carried ship's boats.

All three ships were very shallow, being able to sail in less than 7 feet of water. The area below deck was used to store supplies. The crew slept above deck without even the luxury of a hammock, for this item had not yet been discovered. Instead, each man unrolled a small mat and blanket on the driest corner of the deck he could find.

Wagons West

Objective

Students will use the dimensions of a covered wagon bed to make full-sized chalk replicas on the playground. By circling the wagons, students will also practice determining the circumference of a circle.

What You Need

- sidewalk chalk
- assorted measuring devices (string, rulers, yardsticks, etc.)
- drawing of covered wagon and supplies (see pages 24 and 25)

Before You Begin

The class should read one of the many nonfiction works about pioneers settling the West. Try to find a book that gives details about the actual journey (sleeping quarters, provisions, weapons, furnishings, etc.).

Discuss with the class different ways of measuring a large area: yardstick by yardstick, ruler by ruler, measuring a piece of string or ribbon and then stretching it out, measuring a person's foot and then walking off the dimensions, etc.

What You Do

1. Divide the class into groups of three to five students. Give each group a copy of pages 24 and 25 and several pieces of chalk.

2. As a class, make a large circle on the playground around which the wagons will be drawn. To do this, multiply the number of groups by the length of a covered wagon. This equals the circumference of the circle. Divide the circumference by 3.14 (pi) and you will get the diameter. Divide the diameter in half to equal the radius. Cut a piece of string the length of the radius and make a circle following the instructions on page 10.

Wagons West

3. Each group should choose a measurement method and make a full-sized chalk outline of its wagon.

4. As a class, stand inside the wagon circle. Talk about occasions when the wagons had to be placed in a circle formation.

Things To Think About

Discuss the crowded conditions in the wagons. Ask the students to consider what it must have been like to live on them for more than a month. How do they think the pioneers felt? What discomforts did the pioneers have to endure? Which provisions were essential? What things had to be left behind?

Have students share their personal travel experiences and compare the speed at which cars, buses, trains, and airplanes travel versus covered wagons. How do superhighways compare to the wagon trails?

Challenge

Encourage students to research early American wagons (Conestoga, prairie schooner, stage coach, tinker's wagon). Ask them to draw various types of wagons and their accessories, making their drawings as detailed as possible.

More Ways to Play

Make an actual model of one of the early wagons listed above and label the various parts.

Chalk It Up!
© The Learning Works, Inc.

Wagons West

Circle the Wagons

The sturdy covered wagons used by the pioneers had to be light enough to be pulled easily by oxen, yet sturdy enough to haul loads of up to 2,500 pounds. The best wagons were made from hardwoods such as maple, hickory, and oak. The wheels, hounds, and axles were made from iron. A cloth cover shielded the travelers from the rain and dust.

Draw a rectangle 4 feet wide and 10 feet long on the blacktop to represent your group's wagon. Compute the amount of supplies you will need and fit them within your wagon.

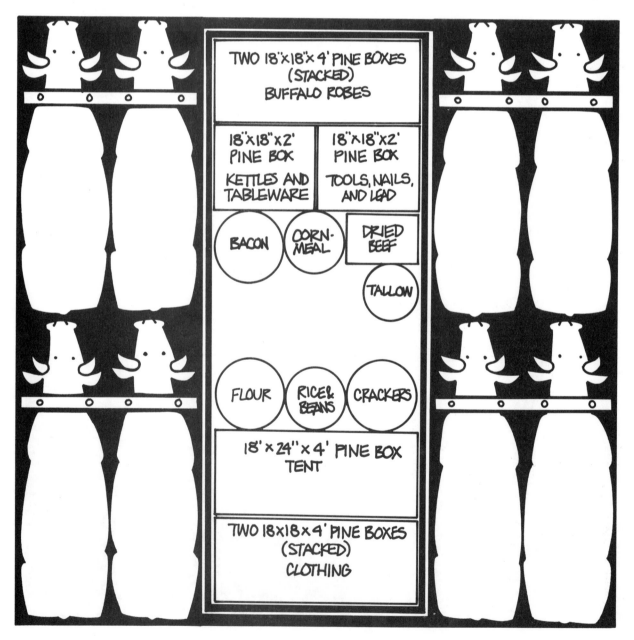

Wagons West

Pack Up Your Wagons

(Supplies for a wagon trip from Independence, Missouri, to Oregon)

Supplies per wagon

- eight strong oxen
- four yokes with extra bows
- ropes and harnesses
- ax
- drawing knife
- handsaw
- set of augers (1/2" to 2")
- gimlet
- hammer
- four pounds of assorted wrought iron nails
- 40 pounds of tallow
- 15 pounds of black lead
- sheet iron camp kettles
- circular tent

Suggested supplies per adult

- 100 pounds of flour
- 100 pounds of butter crackers
- 100 pounds of bacon sides
- 50 pounds of dried beef
- 50 pounds of kiln-dried cornmeal
- 20 pounds of rice
- 25 pounds of beans
- one light rifle
- one small tomahawk
- two pairs of green goggles (for dust)
- tin tableware
- buffalo robes for bedding
- ordinary wearing apparel

Visiting the Old West

Objective

Students will research the buildings of an early western town and, using compass directions, move around the town in an ordered fashion.

What You Need

- sidewalk chalk
- simple designs for various town buildings
- various yardsticks, string, and other tools for drawing straight lines
- library books on frontier towns
- index cards (for hiding treasure)

Before You Begin

Research western towns that existed from approximately 1870–1900. Bring in library books about the settlement of western towns.

Brainstorm buildings and landmarks that might appear in the local setting (schoolhouse, church, bank, post office, boarding house, hotel, stable/livery, general store, cemetery, blacksmith's shop, saloon, doctor's office, etc.).

Make a street plot of the town on the playground using the diagram on page 29. Ask the class to add interesting names to the town's streets.

Determine the scale for the building outlines so that they are in proportion. Find an area that is large enough so that the whole town can be reconstructed in one location.

Visiting the Old West

What You Do

1. Divide the class into teams of two. Have each pair select one building or landmark to design on scratch paper. As a team makes a choice, cross that particular item off the brainstorming list so that the buildings are not duplicated.

2. Pass out chalk and head for the playground.

3. Have the teams draw their buildings in chalk. Write the name of the building or use some symbol to indicate the type of structure, for example, a bell for the schoolhouse or barrels for the store. (Note: You can assign the students to certain lots in the town plot or have a "land grab" and let them race for their spot.)

4. Draw a large compass rose in one corner of the town. Read directions (go southeast 10 steps, etc.) as a pair of students attempts to reach a predetermined destination. This is a fun way to practice compass reading. As the class becomes familiar with the procedure, make the directions more difficult to follow.

5. As a fun conclusion to this lesson, hide a real treasure (watermelon, suckers, stickers) and have the class "locate" it. Fold a number of index cards in half. On one card, write the name of the treat. Leave the other cards blank. Place all of the cards throughout the town. See if the class can locate the card with the name of the treasure. Divide the treat among the class members and enjoy.

Visiting the Old West

Things to Think About

How will you determine what size steps to take so that directions are consistent?

What other ways can you think of to utilize your western town? Consider inviting a primary class to join you in directional games as well.

Challenge

Have students hide an imaginary treasure somewhere within the confines of the town. Then have each student write directions from a given starting point to help classmates reach the "treasure." Encourage students to write creative directions rather than just giving standard compass readings: "Go two doors past the innkeeper's place, then turn clockwise one-fourth turn and cross the street."

More Ways to Play

Draw the interior of a castle.

Draw the layout for a frontier fort.

Visiting the Old West

Example of Street Plot Plan

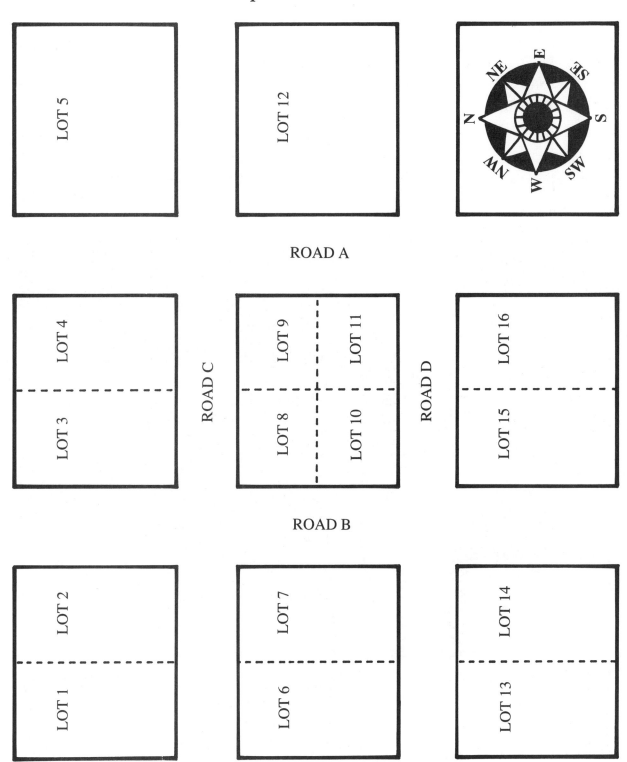

Comparing States

Objective

Students will draw proportional outlines of different states and compare state sizes and shapes as well as dominant geographical features.

What You Need

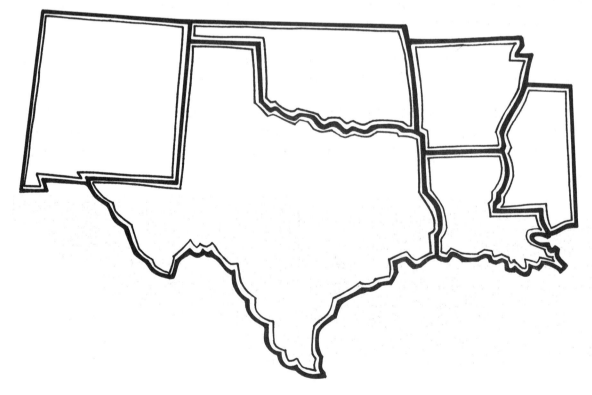

- sidewalk chalk
- string
- scissors
- atlas, almanac, encyclopedia, computer-software reference tools (optional)
- state outlines (pages 33 and 34)

Before You Begin

Have a brief class discussion on how the United States is made up of 50 individual states. Point out that the states were added to the Union over a period of years (from Delaware in 1757 to Hawaii in 1959).

Examine a large map of the United States. Note the diversity of shape and size of the individual states. Forty-eight of the states are contiguous, or touching.

Comparing States

What You Do

1. Divide the class into small groups of three to five students. Let each group pick its favorite state(s) or assign states to the groups.

2. Give the students a copy of the charts on pages 33 and 34. Students should note the size of the state in square miles and round off that number to the nearest thousand.

3. Have the students determine the amount of string needed to outline the state. (Note: To ensure the students draw the states to the same scale, use a formula of 4 inches of string per 1,000 square miles. For example, Ohio is 41,222 square miles and rounds off to 41,000 square miles (41,000 ÷ 1,000 = 41), and 41 x 4 inches = 164 inches of string.

4. Convert inches to yards before measuring the string. In the case of Ohio, 164 inches divided by 36 inches equals 4 yards and 20 inches.

5. Cut the appropriate lengths of string for each group.

6. Referring to the sketch of the state, each group should form an outline of its state on the playground using the string. (Note: It is much easier to form the state outline if you tape the two ends of the string together before you begin.)

7. When the string is arranged to the group's satisfaction, the students should draw a chalk line along the string and then remove the string.

8. Once all of the drawings are complete, the students can examine one another's work and try to identify the states by shape or compare sizes of various states.

9. Teachers can also incorporate other state information into this lesson. Have students draw a star at the location of the state capital, compare the shape and size of their home state to other states, or guess the total number of square miles of the states drawn by classmates.

31

Comparing States

Things to Think About

Discuss how state boundaries came to be. Why does Idaho have a panhandle? Why aren't all states squared off equally? Which state boundaries are affected by the Mississippi River? Are any other state boundaries demarcated by major rivers? Ask students to name other geographical attributes, such as mountains, lakes, and oceans that have helped define state borders.

Remind the students of the variations in the size of the states and then point out that each state has two senators with equal votes in the U.S. Senate. Is this fair? Why or why not? What is the "rule of numbers" for the House of Representatives?

Challenges

Rather than provide the students with the state outlines and square mileage figures, ask each group to research its own data using an encyclopedia, almanac, atlas, or computer software. During the discussion period, determine which reference material was the easiest to use and why.

Have students round the states' area measurements to the nearest hundreds and convert to decimals. Do conversions on paper and check them with a calculator.

Ask the students to draw a small state within a larger state. Have the class determine how many states are smaller than Texas or Alaska and how many of those states could fit within the Texan or Alaskan boundaries at the same time using total area. How many could fit in at one time if their shapes didn't change?

More Ways to Play

As a class, compare notable geographic features in your home state or local area to ones that might not be as well known to your class. For example, students in Utah might compare the Great Salt Lake to Lake Erie.

Have students compare country to country (France to Japan) or country to state (Switzerland to Arkansas).

Comparing States

Shapes and Areas

Students can use the outlines and area figures below or look them up in an atlas or almanac.

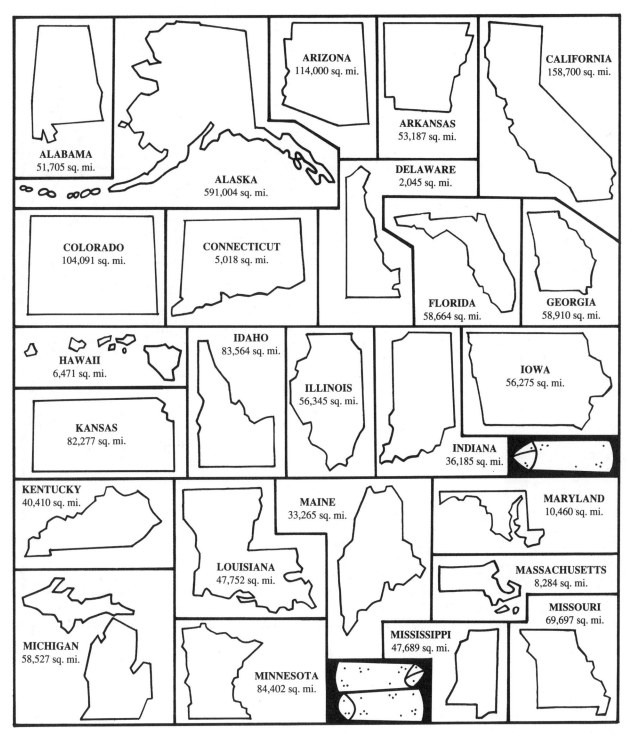

ALABAMA
51,705 sq. mi.

ALASKA
591,004 sq. mi.

ARIZONA
114,000 sq. mi.

ARKANSAS
53,187 sq. mi.

CALIFORNIA
158,700 sq. mi.

DELAWARE
2,045 sq. mi.

COLORADO
104,091 sq. mi.

CONNECTICUT
5,018 sq. mi.

FLORIDA
58,664 sq. mi.

GEORGIA
58,910 sq. mi.

HAWAII
6,471 sq. mi.

IDAHO
83,564 sq. mi.

ILLINOIS
56,345 sq. mi.

IOWA
56,275 sq. mi.

KANSAS
82,277 sq. mi.

INDIANA
36,185 sq. mi.

KENTUCKY
40,410 sq. mi.

MAINE
33,265 sq. mi.

MARYLAND
10,460 sq. mi.

LOUISIANA
47,752 sq. mi.

MASSACHUSETTS
8,284 sq. mi.

MISSOURI
69,697 sq. mi.

MICHIGAN
58,527 sq. mi.

MINNESOTA
84,402 sq. mi.

MISSISSIPPI
47,689 sq. mi.

33

Comparing States

Shapes and Areas

Students can use the outlines and area figures below or look them up in an atlas or almanac.

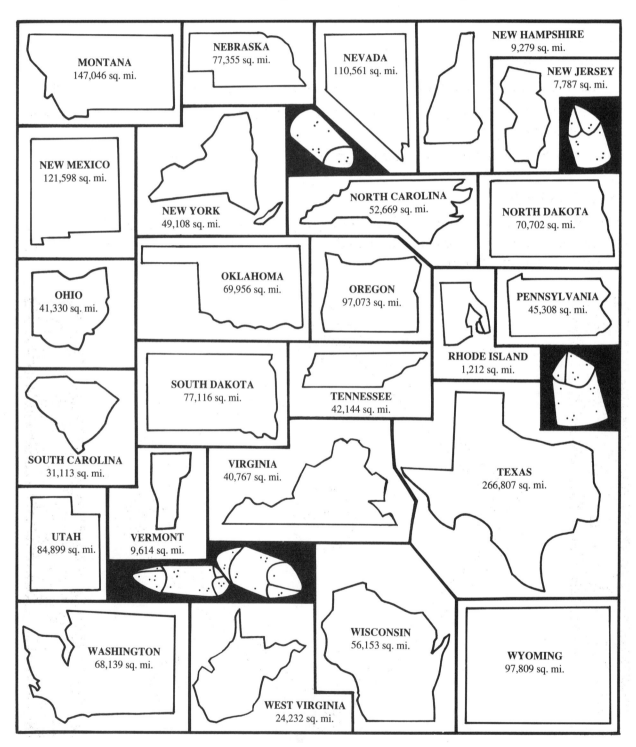

MONTANA
147,046 sq. mi.

NEBRASKA
77,355 sq. mi.

NEVADA
110,561 sq. mi.

NEW HAMPSHIRE
9,279 sq. mi.

NEW JERSEY
7,787 sq. mi.

NEW MEXICO
121,598 sq. mi.

NEW YORK
49,108 sq. mi.

NORTH CAROLINA
52,669 sq. mi.

NORTH DAKOTA
70,702 sq. mi.

OHIO
41,330 sq. mi.

OKLAHOMA
69,956 sq. mi.

OREGON
97,073 sq. mi.

PENNSYLVANIA
45,308 sq. mi.

RHODE ISLAND
1,212 sq. mi.

SOUTH DAKOTA
77,116 sq. mi.

TENNESSEE
42,144 sq. mi.

SOUTH CAROLINA
31,113 sq. mi.

VIRGINIA
40,767 sq. mi.

TEXAS
266,807 sq. mi.

UTAH
84,899 sq. mi.

VERMONT
9,614 sq. mi.

WASHINGTON
68,139 sq. mi.

WISCONSIN
56,153 sq. mi.

WYOMING
97,809 sq. mi.

WEST VIRGINIA
24,232 sq. mi.

Capital Baseball

Objective

Students will practice memorizing state capitals.

What You Need

- sidewalk chalk
- one United States map with each state outline named and numbered (see page 39)
- one United States map with state capitals identified as well as states named and numbered (see page 40)
- a small paper bag with the 50 slips of paper numbered 1 through 50.

Before You Begin

Determine how many innings you are going to play. Each team gets a turn at bat every inning. Make a chalk replica of a baseball diamond on the blacktop approximately 10 feet square (see example below).

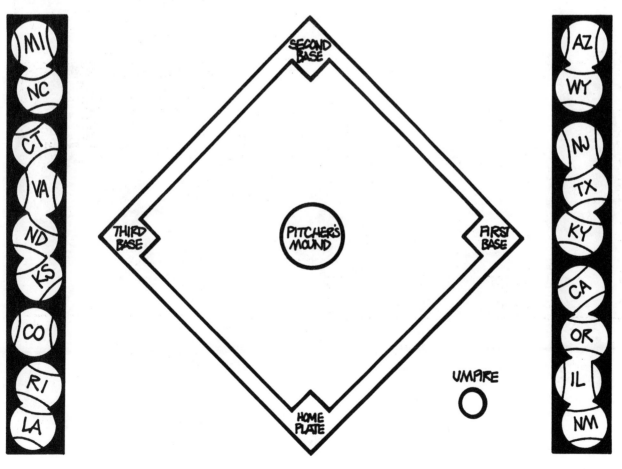

Capital Baseball

What You Do

1. Divide the class into two teams. Appoint a pitcher for each team. Each pitcher draws a number from the bag. The pitcher who draws the highest number gets a choice of being the away team or the home team.

2. Appoint an umpire. Give her a copy of the map with the capitals identified (see page 40).

3. The home-team pitcher takes the bag of numbers and stands on the pitching mound.

4. The first batter on the away team takes the map with state names only (see page 39) and stands at home plate.

5. The batter announces whether he is going to try for a single, a double, a triple, or a home run. If he chooses a single, he must identify one state capital; for a double, two capitals; a triple, three capitals; and for a home run, four capitals. If he makes a mistake, it is an out, and his turn is over.

6. The pitcher pulls out the appropriate number of slips of paper 1, 2, 3, or 4. She reads the numbers printed on the slips to the batter, one at a time.

Capital Baseball

7. Looking at his map, the batter reads the name of the state that has the matching number on it and names its capital. For example, if the pitcher draws number 17, the batter would look at his map and see that Texas is numbered 17. The batter would answer that the capital of Texas is Austin (or whatever he thinks is correct).

8. If the batter is correct, the umpire shouts, "It's a hit!" and the batter moves to the appropriate base. Then the next batter is up. If, however, the batter chooses to try for a double, triple, or home run, he must get all of the answers correct to advance.

9. As hits are made, the batters move around the bases just like regular baseball. For example, if there is a player on first, and the next batter hits a double, the player on first advances to third base, and the batter moves to second. If the third batter hits a triple, both the player on second and the player on third cross home plate (scoring 1 point each for the team). The batter takes his position at third.

10. Each time a player crosses home plate, the team gets a point.

11. If a player misses an answer, the umpire shouts, "You're out!" (Note: You may want to appoint a scorekeeper to keep track of outs and runs.)

12. When a team has three outs or has gone all the way through the batting order one time, it is the other team's turn at bat.

Capital Baseball

Things to Think About

What memory tricks make it easier to remember state capitals? (It's Ohio, Columbus!)

Who resides at the state capital?

What are the three branches of state government? Which one makes the laws? Which one enforces the laws? Which one interprets the laws?

What is the difference between the state capital (the place or city) and the state capitol (the building)?

Challenge

Students play the same game but use a map without the names of the states. Have students identify the state by its shape and name the capital.

More Ways to Play

Students can make their own maps and add famous landmarks and geographic features such as the Rocky Mountains, the Mississippi River, the Great Lakes, and the Grand Canyon.

Have the students identify which of the seven regions the state belongs in (Pacific Coast, Mountain West, South Central, North Central, Middle Atlantic, Southeast, or New England).

Capital Baseball

State Outlines Map

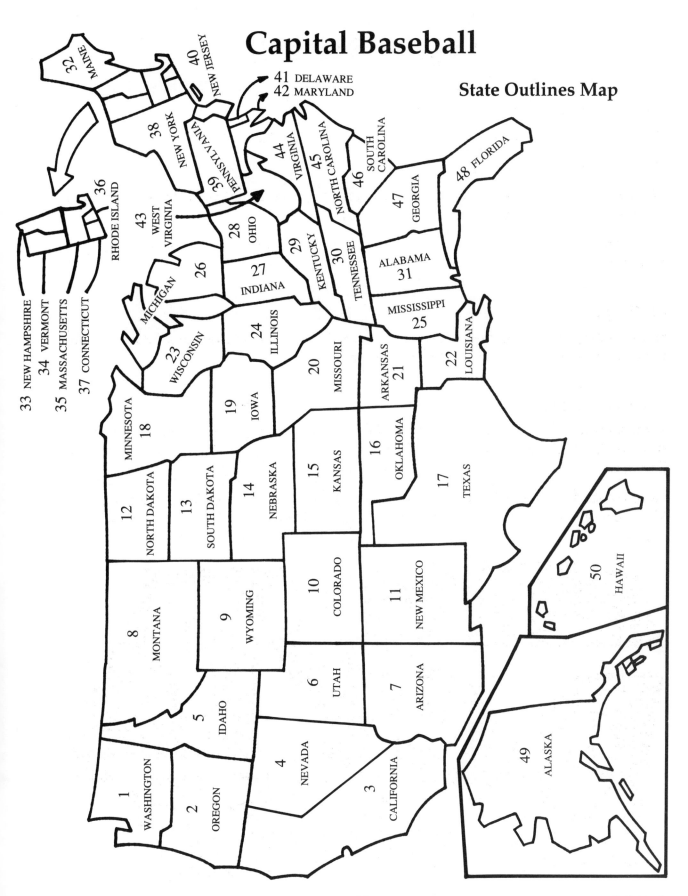

Capital Baseball

State Capitals Map

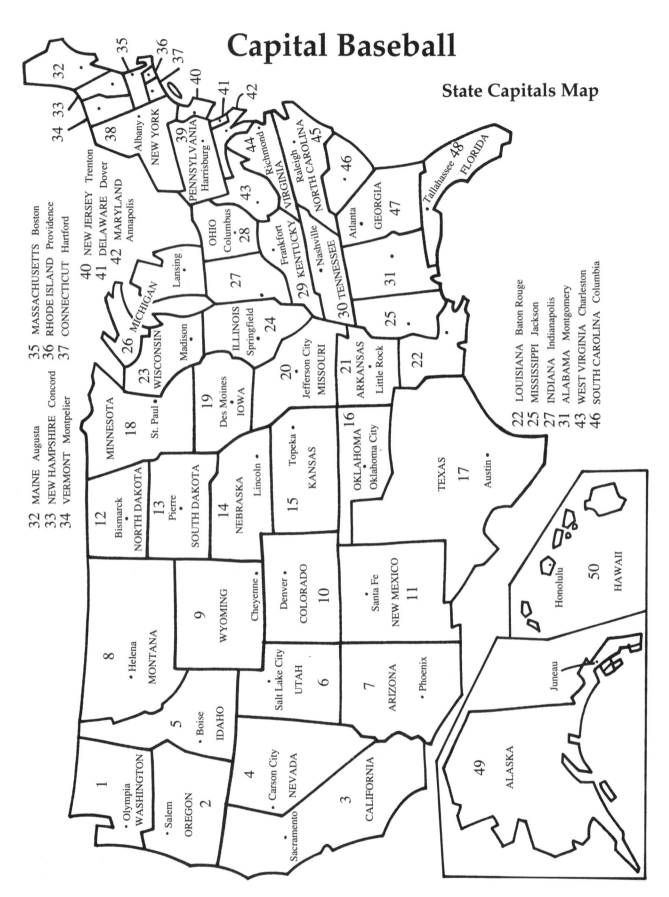

Mapping New Worlds

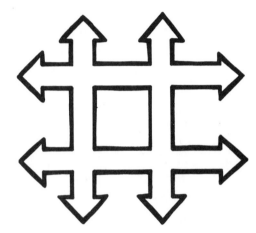

Objective

Students will reinforce the meaning of longitude and latitude by creating a map of an imaginary land on the playground using navigational lines.

What You Need

- sidewalk chalk in various colors
- string to make straight lines
- yardsticks for measuring longitude and latitude
- chalk powder
- scratch paper and pens for each pair of students
- tape measure (for challenge work)

Before You Begin

Discuss what longitude and latitude represent. Study globes and maps and notice the lines of longitude and latitude. Point out that lines (or parallels) of latitude are drawn east and west. Lines (or meridians) of longitude run north and south.

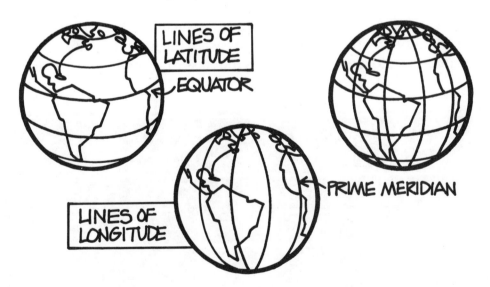

Parallels of latitude are marked in degrees north and south of the equator. The O degree meridian is the Prime Meridian and it runs through Greenwich, England, near London. Longitude lines are marked in degrees east and west of the Prime Meridian. By looking at the meridians, a person can determine which of two countries is farther east.

Mapping New Worlds

What You Do

1. Square off an area of the playground. As a class, create an imaginary continent within that area. Incorporate any fixtures that already exist: for instance, a swing set could become the Insurmountable Mountains, the sand box the Blazing Desert, the grass field the country of Green Fields, and the tetherball pole Striker's Island. Using chalk, draw in additional features such as lakes, swamps, cities, and rivers. See pages 44–45 for a list of features that might be included. Be sure to write down the names of each feature.

2. Using powdered chalk and string, make a line across the bottom of your land and another line up the side. (See page 11 for instructions on how to make straight lines with string.)

3. Mark off the degrees longitude and the degrees latitude using a yardstick. (See the example on the following page.)

4. Working in pairs, students locate which features/countries can be found at a series of points where longitude and latitude lines intersect. One person can stand at the longitude point and walk forward, while the other person stands at the latitude point and walks forward. The intersection point is the place where they meet.

5. Give each pair a list of other things to determine, such as what lake is located farthest north of the equator or which city is farthest east of the mountain range. You will need to vary the questions to match the features the class drew on their land map. Set a time limit.

Mapping New Worlds

6. Each pair writes its answers on a sheet of paper.

7. The game is won by the pair of students that gets the most right answers in the least amount of time.

Things to Think About

When creating an imaginary land, what kinds of questions must you consider (terrain, shape, population centers, etc.)?

Visualize where your land might be located on the globe. Based on this condition, what would its climate be like? How would climate affect your drawing?

Challenge

Make a map of your imaginary land. Determine the scale and develop a measurement tool. Develop a legend for the map.

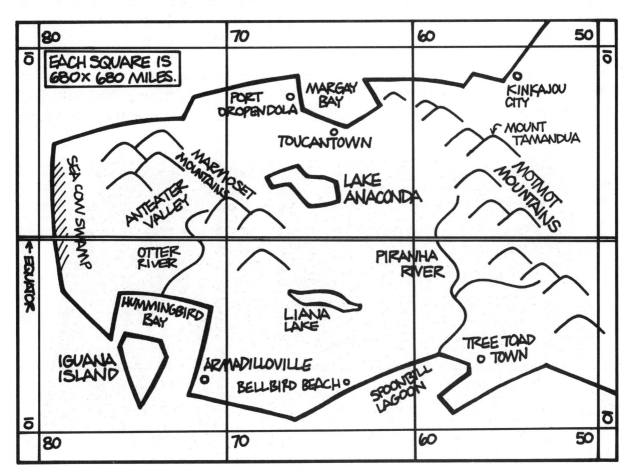

43

Mapping New Worlds

Geographical Terms

bay	an extension of a sea or ocean into the land
butte	an isolated hill or small mountain with steep sides and a small flat top
canal	a man-made channel of water used for passage of ships or for irrigation
cape	a point of land projecting into a sea or an ocean
country	the territory or land occupied by a nation of people
desert	a region made barren by lack of precipitation
fjord	a narrow inlet of sea with steep banks usually formed by a glacier
forest	a large thick growth of trees and underbrush
glacier	a huge mass of ice originating from compact snow
gulf	a large part of an ocean or sea that extends into the land
hill	land higher than lowlands with gentle slopes; shorter than a mountain
isthmus	a narrow strip of land connecting two larger land masses
lagoon	a shallow sound, channel or pond near a larger body of water
lake	a large inland body of water
lowland	low and level land usually found near the oceans or in river valleys

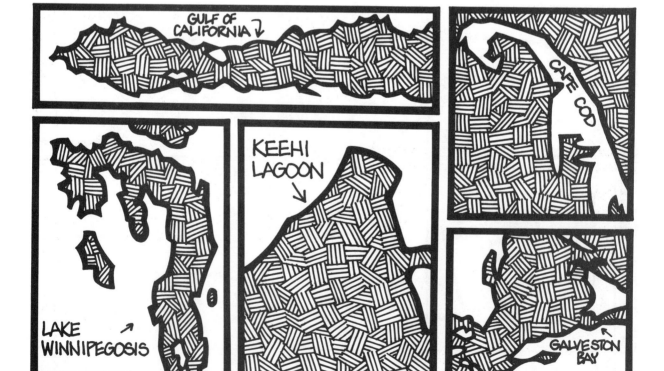

Mapping New Worlds

mountain	a high rocky land with steep sides
mountain range	a group of mountains
ocean	the vast expanse of salt water that covers nearly three-fourths of the surface of the earth; or any one of its five great divisions
peninsula	a long projection of land into water, connected to the mainland by an isthmus
plateau	a region of high flat land
prairie	a large level tract of grassland
rain forest	a tropical woodland that has an annual rainfall of at least 100 inches and is marked by a canopy of large broad-leaved evergreen trees
rapids	usually a shallow part of a river with a fast current
reef	a ridge of rock or sand at or near the surface of the water
river	a natural stream larger than a brook
river delta	a wide alluvial mouth of a river
sound	a body of water separating one or more islands from the mainland
swamp	a wet, spongy land sometimes partially underwater
wetlands	a boggy land saturated with enough ground water to support vegetation

Chalk It Up!
© The Learning Works, Inc.

What's New in the News?

Objective
Students will use headlines from the newspaper to practice extemporaneous speaking.

What You Need
- sidewalk chalk
- newspaper articles collected by students
- one construction-paper square numbered consecutively for each member of the class

Before You Begin
Bring to class some newspaper articles with catchy headlines. Read a headline to the class. Have the students guess what the story will be about. Then read aloud important information that was actually included in the article. Practice this process a number of times.

What You Do

1. Ask each class member to go through a newspaper and pick an article that interests her or him (or pertains to something being studied in class). Have students cut out the full article.

2. Pass out a piece of chalk to each student and head for the playground. Choose a large area and have the class form a circle. Allow plenty of space for each student to work.

3. Have each student chalk in the headline that he or she brought from home. Remind the class to use large printing or handwriting to make the work readable.

What's New in the News?

4. Number off the class and have students put their names and numbers beside their headlines.

5. When headlines are completed, have the class gather together. Have each member of the class take turns drawing a number from a basket. The person goes to the headline matching the number drawn, reads the headline aloud, and then tells the class what he or she thinks the story will be about. When the student is finished, the actual article is shared.

6. Continue until each member of the class has a chance to share. (Note: This lesson may take more than one day.)

Things to Think About

Do the headlines always give an accurate or complete picture of the story?

What parts of speech are usually found in a headline?

How many words typically make up a headline?

How does the size of headline type vary?

Challenges

Have students rewrite the headline to describe the article more accurately. Ask them to try writing headlines using alliteration, where all the words start with the same sound.

Pick important headlines of the week and have students memorize basic facts to share with the class. (Cue cards may or may not be allowed. Make your own rules.)

More Ways to Play

Have students pick a short article and write two headlines on the blacktop along with the headline that appeared in the newspaper. The student should then read the article out loud. Have the rest of the class guess which of the three headlines is the original.

Traveling Through Space

Objective
Students will use the dimensions of the mid deck of a space shuttle orbiter to make full-sized chalk diagrams on the playground.

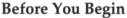

What You Need
- sidewalk chalk
- assorted measuring devices (string, rulers, yardsticks, etc.)
- reference materials with pictures and information on space travel

Before You Begin
Have the class read a nonfiction book about space travel. Try to find a book that includes details about the inside of a space craft. Where did the astronauts go to the bathroom? How did they eat? How much room did they have to stow personal belongings?

What You Do
1. Divide the class into groups of at least seven students (the number of astronauts on a shuttle flight). Give each group a copy of page 49 and several pieces of chalk.

2. Assign each group of students to a separate area of the playground.

3. Each group should make a full-sized chalk outline of the mid deck. Students should then "furnish" their mid decks with chalk-drawn shapes representing the following items/areas:

   - multilevel sleep stations (beds)
   - bathroom
   - kitchen
   - laboratory
   - storage lockers

4. Groups should then move about on their "decks" performing the daily activities of space travel.

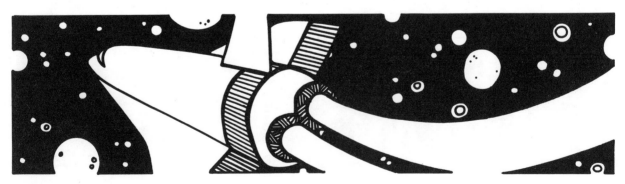

Traveling Through Space

Inside a Shuttle Orbiter

The part of a space shuttle that separates from the booster rockets, orbits the earth, and returns is called the orbiter. On the outside, an orbiter looks like a passenger jet. Inside, the quarters aren't quite as roomy. The crew cabin has three levels. The flight deck is on the first level. It consists of the forward flight deck or cockpit where the commander and the pilot sit. There are over 2,020 separate displays and controls. The mid deck is below the flight deck and measures 10 feet (3 meters) long by 11 feet (3.3 meters) wide. The crew of seven uses this small space as a kitchen, bedroom, bathroom, office, exercise area, and laboratory. The last level is the utility level and houses the life-support systems. This is also where the crew stores its garbage.

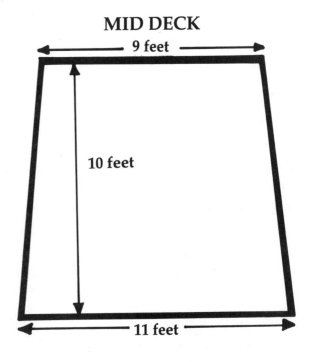

MID DECK

9 feet

10 feet

11 feet

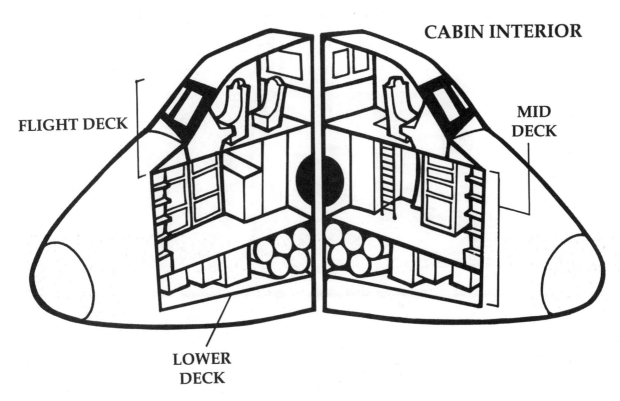

CABIN INTERIOR

FLIGHT DECK

MID DECK

LOWER DECK

49

Traveling Through Space

Things to Think About

Discuss the hardships of being confined in a spacecraft for an extended period of time and the potential dangers astronauts face.

What special considerations have to be made to handle food, to exercise, to dispose of waste, and so forth?

Challenge

Have students research one of the astronauts who has flown on a space shuttle flight. Find out more details about his or her particular space flight. Select one important discovery or experiment associated with the flight.

Star Appeal

Objective
Students will research a star constellation and reproduce it on the playground in chalk.

What You Need
- sidewalk chalk
- scratch paper

Before You Begin
Bring in plenty of books on astronomy as reference materials. Talk about the stars, planets, comets, etc. seen in the night sky.

Have students research various constellations and sketch them on scratch paper.

What You Do

1. Divide the class into groups of two or three students. Using the students' drawings of constellations or the illustrations on pages 53–54, have each group pick one star formation to reproduce on the playground.

2. Pass out chalk and go to the playground. Find an area large enough for all the groups to work without being crowded.

3. Each group should draw a simple arrangement of chalk stars to represent its constellation. It is not necessary to draw the shape around the stars. However, doing so helps reinforce the arrangement of the stars. Be sure to have the students label each constellation so other classes can enjoy the finished drawings.

4. Have the class walk to each constellation so that the creators can share their work.

Star Appeal

Things To Think About

How did sailors use the stars to navigate?

Why are certain stars visible some nights and not visible other nights?

Do people of all nations see the same star formations that we see in our country?

Challenges

Ask students to write a tale or legend to go along with their constellation.

Have students construct a new constellation of their own design, name it, and write an original story to accompany it.

As a class project, cover a wall in the classroom with dark blue or black construction paper. Using foil stars, reproduce the various constellations (real and created) for a classroom display.

Star Appeal

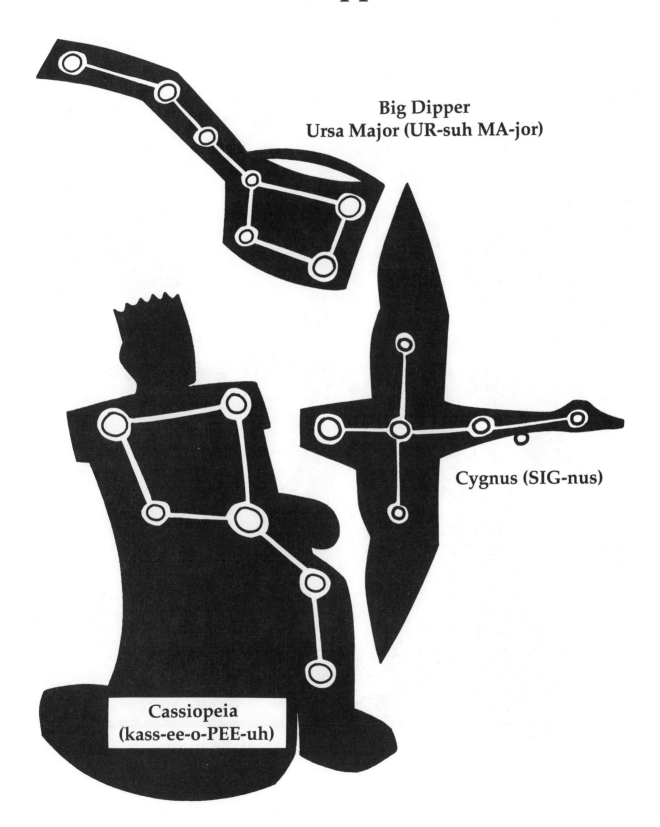

Big Dipper
Ursa Major (UR-suh MA-jor)

Cygnus (SIG-nus)

Cassiopeia
(kass-ee-o-PEE-uh)

Chalk It Up!
© The Learning Works, Inc.

Star Appeal

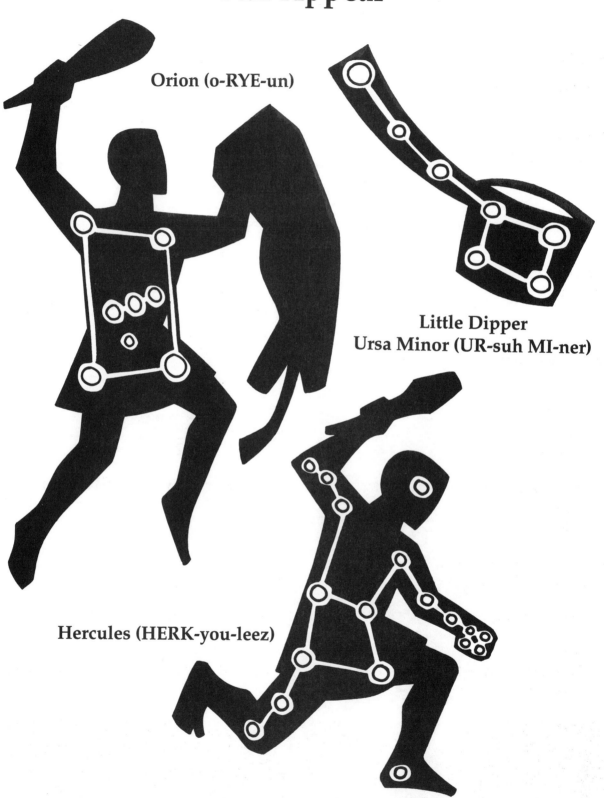

Orion (o-RYE-un)

Little Dipper
Ursa Minor (UR-suh MI-ner)

Hercules (HERK-you-leez)

Design a Dinosaur

Objective

Students will design their own chalk dinosaurs on the playground.

What You Need

- sidewalk chalk
- butcher paper
- encyclopedias, computer software, library books, and other reference tools for dinosaurs

Before You Begin

Using butcher paper, the whole class begins by brainstorming and recording known information about dinosaurs and how they lived. Discuss herbivores versus carnivores.

Using reference tools such as encyclopedias, library books, and computer software, record data about habitat, food chains, offspring, and predators.

What You Do

1. Working in groups or as individuals, students design their own dinosaurs using ideas from the brainstorming session.

2. Have each group define the defense mechanisms and eating habits of its dinosaur. Where would it live? What range of temperature variations could it endure? Would it migrate?

3. Translate those "findings" into physical features. For example, if a dinosaur is a meat eater, it will need large teeth and jaws to tear through the hide of its prey.

4. Determine how big the adult members of the group's dinosaur species would be.

5. Sketch the dinosaur to scale on the playground. To ensure that all the dinosaurs are drawn to the same scale, each group should compute the measurements of its dinosaur using a ratio of six inches per foot.

Design a Dinosaur

Things to Think About

Have scientists discovered all there is to know about dinosaurs? How limited are we by the archeological evidence that remains? What things might dinosaurs have been capable of doing that scientists cannot discover from their bones?

Challenge

Have the students write encyclopedia entries for their dinosaurs. They should include as much information as possible. Which prehistoric dinosaurs would have been enemies of their dinosaurs? Which prehistoric dinosaurs would have been food for them? Why? Ask the students to describe the difference between an encyclopedia entry and a dictionary entry. Have them also write dictionary entries for their dinosaurs.

More Ways to Play

This lesson format can be modified to suit your curriculum. Instead of designing a dinosaur, students could design:

- a creature that might live in the future
- a creature that evolved in a polluted world
- an animal that survived in a particular geographic region, such as Antarctica, a desert, or an ocean

Sundials and Shadows

Objective

Students will show how ancient cultures measured time by using shadows cast by the sun.

What You Need

- sidewalk chalk
- a sunny day

Before You Begin

Brainstorm with your class all of the possible ways to tell time. Discuss the sundials and clocks used by ancient cultures.

What You Do

1. Draw a long line on the playground running east and west. (See page 11 for instructions on how to make a straight line with chalk powder and string.)

2. Have one student stand in the middle of the line. Draw a bar across the line at the end of her shadow. Mark the time of day.

3. Every hour, go back out and have the student stand at the same beginning point. Mark where her shadow crosses the line and note the time of day.

Sundials and Shadows

Things to Think About

At what time of day are the lines closest to the center?

What are the disadvantages of a sun clock?

When or where would you not want to use one?

If you didn't have a sun clock or a watch, how could you determine the approximate time of day using shadows?

What impact does daylight savings time have on sun clocks?

Challenge

Have students research sun clocks designed by the ancient Egyptians as well as the early Greeks and Romans. Design your own structure for marking time by the sun.

Swinging Through the Rain Forest

Objective

Students will learn to identify and classify the various layers of a rain forest as well as the numerous animals that make their habitats there.

What You Need

- colored sidewalk chalk
- reference books and encyclopedias on the rain forest

Before You Begin

Talk about the various layers of a rain forest. Discuss how each layer is a separate ecological system and is the habitat for different animals.

As a class, reproduce the sketch of the rain forest on the playground. At a minimum, mark off the different layers (emergent trees, upper canopy, lower canopy, and understory). Students can copy the design on page 62, sketch their own trees and plants, or simply make a column with each section marked in a different color. Don't worry about artistic ability. It is more important that the students get a feeling for the height of the different levels rather than drawing a realistic-looking rain forest.

Assign each student an animal(s) to research. (See pages 63–64 for a list of possible animals.) Students should find out as much as they can about their animal and determine in which part of the rain forest it lives. Also they should find out if that is the only environment in which it can be found and whether or not it is an endangered species.

Swinging Through the Rain Forest

What You Do

1. Have each student write a first-person story describing the animal from the animal's point of view. Pretending to be that animal, a student explains what it eats, where it lives, how it reproduces, etc.

2. When a student has finished writing his or her story, he or she should stand on the diagram in the appropriate layer of the rain forest where his or her animal lives.

3. When all of the students are in place, have them read their stories. Those who represent animals that would become extinct if the rain forest were destroyed should leave the diagram when they finish.

Things To Thing About

What is the difference between a threatened species, an endangered species, and an extinct species?

Can humans live in a world without animals?

How can people in the United States contribute to saving rain forests and rain forest animals in other countries? Should global considerations take precedent over the needs of individual countries?

Swinging Through the Rain Forest

Challenge

Instead of standing on the diagram, students can draw pictures of the animals. Students may research more than one animal. When all of the animals have been drawn, have the students place large red Xs on those animals that would become extinct if the rain forest were destroyed.

More Ways to Play

Have students research rain forest plants as well as animals. Sketch the plants on the diagram and label them. Find out which plants are used for medicinal purposes. What other rain forest plants can be used by man? Tropical fruit trees (coconut, guava, banana, star fruit), nut trees, and plants that yield spices (cinnamon, nutmeg, cloves, curry) are some examples.

Compare temperate and tropical rain forests. Research their temperature and humidity. How do they compare? How do they differ? Name the different animals and plants that can be found in the various layers of a temperate rain forest.

Swinging Through the Rain Forest

Rain Forest Strata

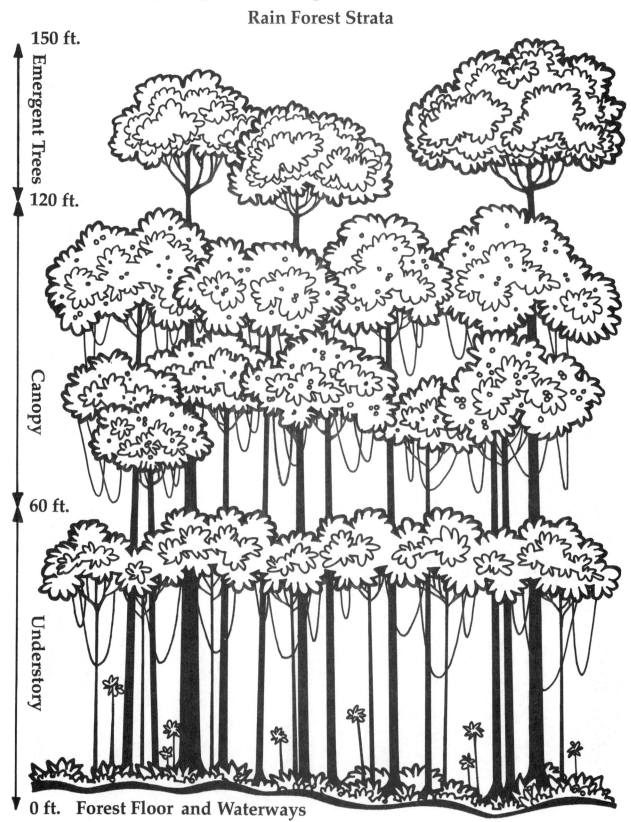

150 ft.

Emergent Trees

120 ft.

Canopy

60 ft.

Understory

0 ft. Forest Floor and Waterways

Swinging Through the Rain Forest

Residents of the Rain Forest

Rain forests are home to approximately half of all plant and animal species on the earth. The following is a partial list of the animals that can be found in most tropical rain forests. They vary depending on the location of the rain forest. The animals are listed under the rain forest layer in which they are primarily found. For instance, the three-toed sloth lives almost exclusively in the upper canopy except for weekly visits to the ground to defecate.

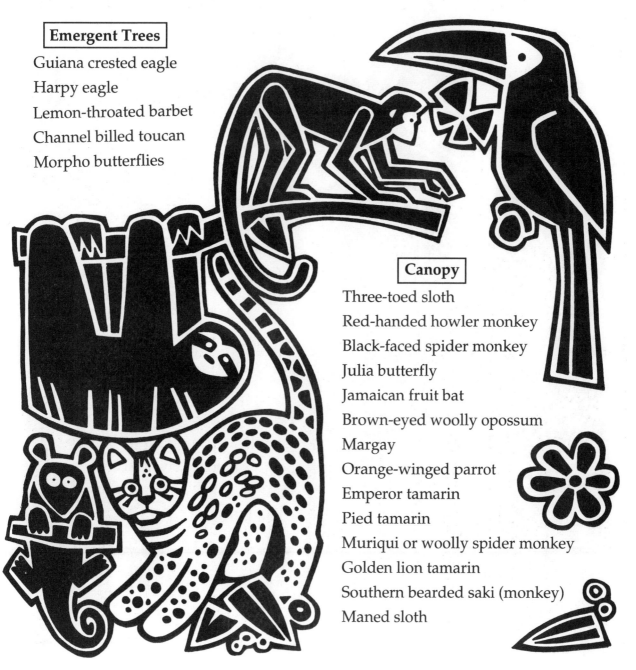

Emergent Trees

Guiana crested eagle

Harpy eagle

Lemon-throated barbet

Channel billed toucan

Morpho butterflies

Canopy

Three-toed sloth

Red-handed howler monkey

Black-faced spider monkey

Julia butterfly

Jamaican fruit bat

Brown-eyed woolly opossum

Margay

Orange-winged parrot

Emperor tamarin

Pied tamarin

Muriqui or woolly spider monkey

Golden lion tamarin

Southern bearded saki (monkey)

Maned sloth

63

Swinging Through the Rain Forest

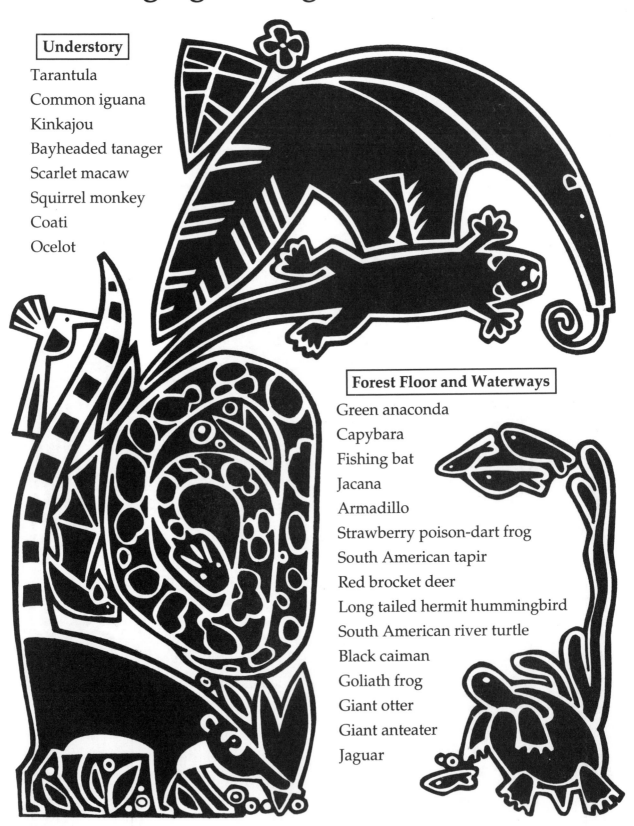

Understory

Tarantula

Common iguana

Kinkajou

Bayheaded tanager

Scarlet macaw

Squirrel monkey

Coati

Ocelot

Forest Floor and Waterways

Green anaconda

Capybara

Fishing bat

Jacana

Armadillo

Strawberry poison-dart frog

South American tapir

Red brocket deer

Long tailed hermit hummingbird

South American river turtle

Black caiman

Goliath frog

Giant otter

Giant anteater

Jaguar

Whales of Fun

Objective

Students will learn about whales and compare the range in sizes of these denizens of the deep as they draw various species on the playground.

What You Need

- sidewalk chalk
- various reference books on whales
- illustrations of whales (see pages 67–70)

Before You Begin

Divide the class into groups. Assign each group a different species of whale. The group should research its whale and find out its distinguishing physical features, behavior, diet, breeding habits, migration route or location in the world, major predators, and present status (extinct, endangered, threatened, etc.).

What You Do

1. Using their own illustrations or those on pages 67–70, the groups should meet on the playground and sketch a life-sized outline of their whale on the blacktop.

2. Below their drawing, each group should write their whale's name, size, and status.

3. Have group members share with the class all the information they learned about their species of whale.

Chalk It Up!
© The Learning Works, Inc.

Whales of Fun

Things to Think About

Which whale was the largest?

How many students can fit in the belly of the largest whale? How many can fit in the belly of the smallest whale?

What purpose do whales serve in the natural environment? What would happen if all of the whales disappeared?

Challenges

Have students do research to find out how large a baby whale of their group's species would be and then draw it next to the mother whale.

Ask students to calculate how many cars or other modern conveniences it would take to equal the weight of an adult whale.

Whales of Fun

Baleen Whales

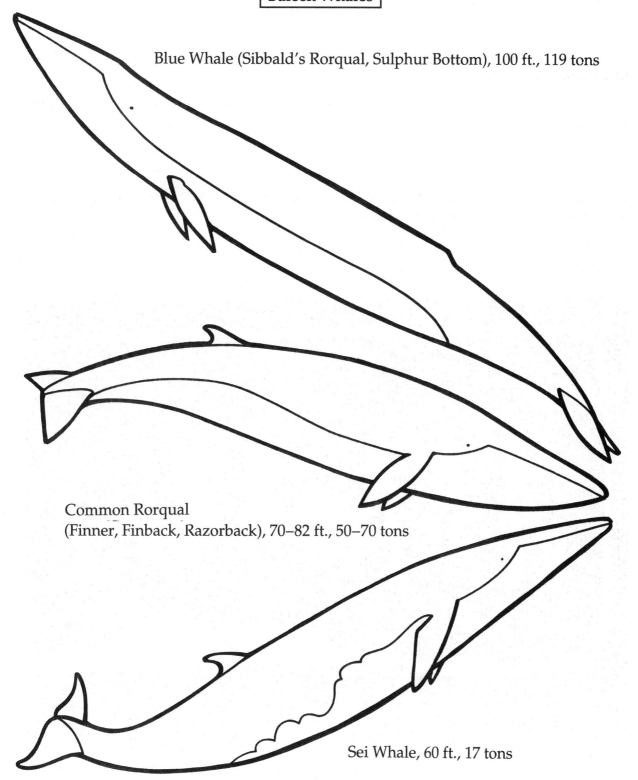

Blue Whale (Sibbald's Rorqual, Sulphur Bottom), 100 ft., 119 tons

Common Rorqual
(Finner, Finback, Razorback), 70–82 ft., 50–70 tons

Sei Whale, 60 ft., 17 tons

Whales of Fun

Baleen Whales

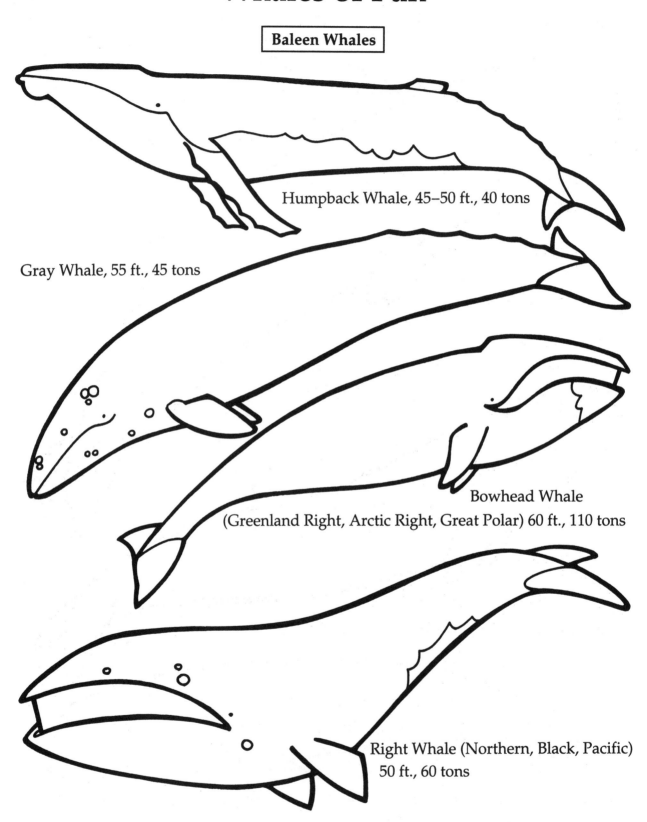

Humpback Whale, 45–50 ft., 40 tons

Gray Whale, 55 ft., 45 tons

Bowhead Whale
(Greenland Right, Arctic Right, Great Polar) 60 ft., 110 tons

Right Whale (Northern, Black, Pacific)
50 ft., 60 tons

Whales of Fun

Toothed Whales

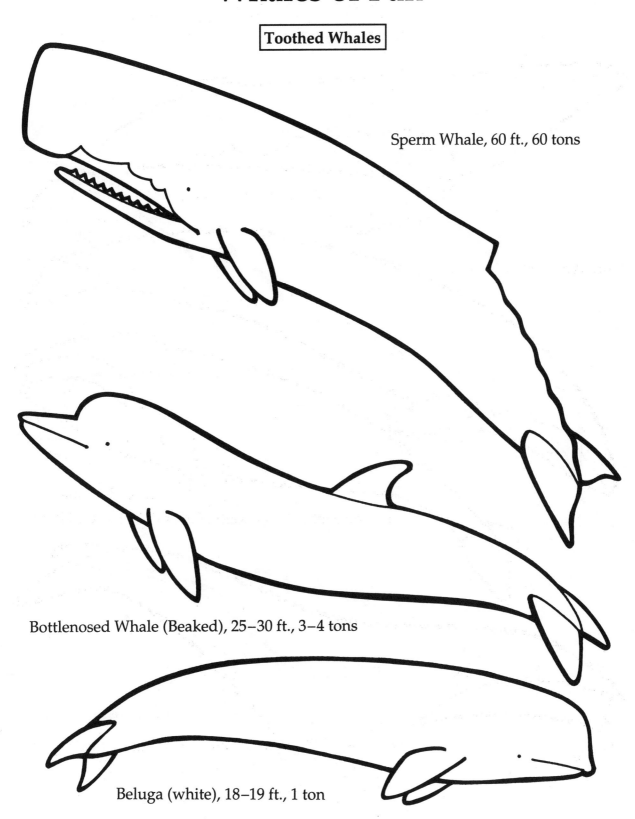

Sperm Whale, 60 ft., 60 tons

Bottlenosed Whale (Beaked), 25–30 ft., 3–4 tons

Beluga (white), 18–19 ft., 1 ton

69

Whales of Fun

Toothed Whales

Killer Whale, 30 ft., 8 tons

Pilot Whale, 19–26 ft., 4 tons

Narwhal, 13–18 ft. (without tusk), 1.8 tons

Parts of Flowering Plants

Objective

Students will study the parts of a plant and will chalk the plant diagram on the playground.

What You Need

- sidewalk chalk
- pictures of plants
- diagram of plant parts on page 73

Before You Begin

Brainstorm with the class all the words that have to do with plants (roots, soil, bud, stem, leaves, stalk, bulb, seeds, fertilizer, petal, blossom, etc.) Circle all the words on the list that are plant parts.

Have each student pick a flowering plant and research it.

What You Do

1. Pair off the students. Each pair of students should choose one of the two plants they have researched as the plant they will draw.

2. Pass out chalk and head for the playground. Assign a work area for each pair.

3. Using their research materials and the sample diagram on page 73, the students should draw and label the parts of their plants. Be sure the students add the name of the plant at the top of their drawings.

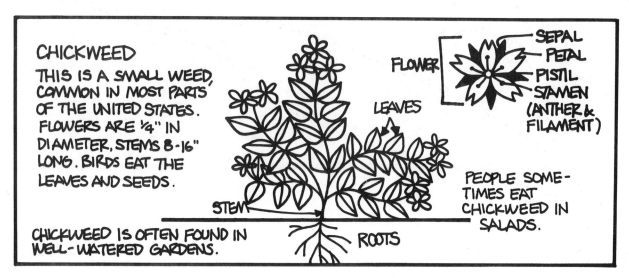

CHICKWEED

THIS IS A SMALL WEED, COMMON IN MOST PARTS OF THE UNITED STATES. FLOWERS ARE ¼" IN DIAMETER, STEMS 8-16" LONG. BIRDS EAT THE LEAVES AND SEEDS.

CHICKWEED IS OFTEN FOUND IN WELL-WATERED GARDENS.

FLOWER

LEAVES

STEM

ROOTS

SEPAL
PETAL
PISTIL
STAMEN
(ANTHER & FILAMENT)

PEOPLE SOME-TIMES EAT CHICKWEED IN SALADS.

Parts of Flowering Plants

Things to Think About

Do all plants have the same parts?

Which plants start from seeds? Which start from bulbs?

What important function is provided by each part of the plant?

Do all plants need sunlight?

Should you water a plant daily?

Is it important to fertilize plants?

Do bug sprays help the plant? Is the environment hurt by bug sprays?

Challenge

Have each student do additional research on the plant he or she has drawn to determine the following information: How deep would you plant your seed or bulb? How much moisture is necessary to maintain a healthy plant? How much sun exposure is good for your plant? What temperature is ideal for your plant? Is it an outdoor or an indoor plant? In what habitat would you find your plant growing? Do any animals use your type of plant for food or shelter?

Parts of Flowering Plants

Labeling the Parts of a Flowering Plant

Draw a chalk diagram of the flowering plant that you researched. Using the example below, identify and label the major parts.

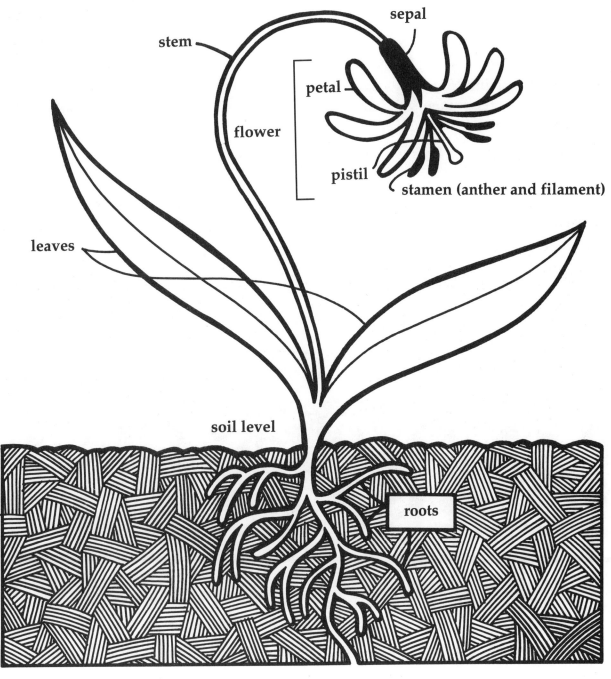

Chalking Longfellow

Objective

Students will practice poetry on the playground using alliteration and couplets.

What You Need

- sidewalk chalk
- one dictionary per team or individual student

Before You Begin

Review various kinds of poetry. Have class members bring in as many poetry books as possible. Encourage students to share favorite poems with the class. (This is a wonderful way to begin or end the day.)

Introduce couplets (two lines with rhyming last words). Discuss the meaning of alliteration.

What You Do

1. Divide the class into teams.

2. Have each team pick two letters from the alphabet.

3. Head for the playground and assign working space (5' x 5') on the cement or blacktop.

4. Each team compiles a list of words (nouns, verbs, adjectives, adverbs, etc.) that begins with its chosen letters and writes them in chalk in the assigned space.

Chalking Longfellow

5. Using their list of words, team members begin to form a phrase or sentence using as many words with the same beginning letter as possible. They should make sure each word also begins with the same sound. For example, "A lazy lion laps lukewarm liquid from a lacy leaf."

6. Next, have the students put together a second sentence, using the other letter they chose. The last word of the second line should rhyme with the last word of the first line. They are now forming alliterative couplets.

    Example:

    "A lazy lion laps lukewarm liquid from a lacy leaf,
    Charming a chuckling chimpanzee as she challenges the chief."

7. Ask students to use the dictionary to check spelling and/or correct any errors.

8. Share the verses aloud. Students should be able to define any of the words that they use. Encourage humor and originality.

Things to Think About

Does all poetry have to rhyme?

Is alliteration an effective way to express feelings? Why or why not? If two words begin with the same letter, are they always alliterative? When are they alliterative and when are they not?

Is poetry composition easier as a team effort or would individual work be more satisfying?

Challenges

Have students write phrases alternating their chosen letters to start each word. For example, "Kate's perky kitten preferred kidney pies."

Have students select words that are not readily familiar. Classmates should try to guess the meaning of the words using context clues.

Ask the class to research poems that use alliteration. Have students memorize them and share them with the rest of the class.

Adjective Action

Objective

Students will practice selecting and using descriptive adjectives by observing their outdoor surroundings.

What You Need

- sidewalk chalk in various colors
- dictionary (for challenges)
- a watch or timer

Before You Begin

Discuss the purpose of adjectives in writing (to give more imagery to your thoughts). Brainstorm adjective categories such as color words, size words, and shape words. Explain how adjectives differ from adverbs, nouns, verbs, or other parts of speech.

What You Do

1. Divide the class into groups. Pass out chalk. Find a spot where the groups can work close to each other.

2. Set a time limit, and have the groups list as many adjectives as they can within a three to five minute period. The adjectives must be descriptive of something the students can observe from where they are seated (green grass, puffy clouds, tall trees, etc.).

3. At the end of the time limit, have a member from each group read aloud the adjectives from his or her group's list. If another group has any of the same adjectives, they must be crossed off all lists. When all lists have been read, the teams get one point for each adjective remaining on their list.

4. If a group wishes to challenge a word on another group's list, its members may check the word in the dictionary. If the word is not an adjective, the challengers get an extra point and the word must be crossed off the list. If the word is an adjective, the challengers lose a point, and the group who came up with the word gets a bonus point along with the original point for that word.

5. A group can also challenge an adjective that it does not believe can be "seen." For example, if the word was "puffy," the group might defend it by pointing to the puffy clouds. Points are awarded or subtracted as in number 4. The teacher is the final judge.

Adjective Action

6. Words must be spelled correctly. Deduct a half a point for misspelled words.

7. The team with the most points wins.

Things to Think About

What methods might help increase the length of the list?

Should adjectives be named at random or should nouns be looked at individually (blade of grass: green, slender, short, wavy, etc.)?

Should there be one recorder or should all students record?

Should the group appoint its best speller to proof words before the time limit is up?

Challenges

Form sentences using all of the adjectives that remained on each list. Write the sentence so that the adjectives are illustrated. *Blue* would be in blue chalk, *bumpy* might be written

and jagged could be written

Select one or two letters and make all of the adjectives begin with or have within them the selected letter. For example, given the letter "b," students could use blue or billowy, as well as rubber or tubular.

More Ways to Play

Repeat this activity using strategies discussed in class. Be sure the class sits in a different area of the playground so that the students aren't "seeing" the same adjectives.

Letter Maze

Objective

Students will spell as many words as possible from a given maze of letters.

What You Need

- sidewalk chalk
- word maze (drawn on playground)
- scratch paper and pencil
- book (to support paper)
- watch or timer
- a dictionary

Before You Begin

Encourage students to look at objects from different angles and perspectives. Talk about finding words in a letter maze. In a maze, letters may be arranged diagonally, top to bottom, bottom to top, right to left, etc. Practice a few word mazes on the blackboard.

What You Do

1. Pick any 16 letters at random. Be sure to include some vowels.

2. Have one student draw a large maze on the playground using the selected letters. (The other students should not watch the creation of the maze.) The maze should be designed in four rows of four letters each. Be sure the letters are lined up carefully. (If you have a large class, you may need more than one maze.)

Sample Maze

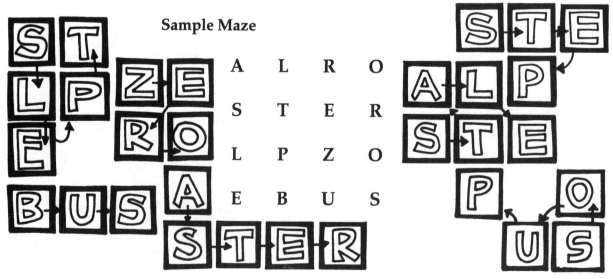

A	L	R	O
S	T	E	R
L	P	Z	O
E	B	U	S

Letter Maze

3. Ask students to find as many words as possible in the maze. Students may move through the maze in any direction, but all of the letters in the word must be adjacent. Plurals are allowed in any maze that contains an "s." A possible word list for the sample maze on page 78 includes *bus, step, zero, sore, last, err, alter, salt, belts, error, later, stereo,* and *belt*. A letter may be used more than once in the same word, as in the word *taste,* but students may not repeat a letter, as in *taller,* unless the letters are adjacent to each other as in the word *error.*

4. Have the students line up with a pencil, scratch paper, and a book to support the paper. Head for the playground and stand around the previously drawn chalk mazes.

5. When the teacher says "Start," the students have three to five minutes to write down as many words as they can see. Words must be spelled correctly.

6. At the end of the given time, the students exchange papers and check the words. Students can use dictionaries if there is a question about the legitimacy of a word or its spelling.

Things to Think About

Is it hard to spot words that are positioned in an unusual manner?

What do you have to think about when creating a letter maze (for example, using common letters, including enough vowels, spacing the vowels, etc.)?

Challenges

Make mazes with more letters (six across and six down).

Try making mazes with numbers instead of letters or write mathematical sentences. You will have to add mathematical signs (+, −, x, ÷, and =).

More Ways to Play

Create an oversized letter maze and have the students "walk" out the words by stepping from letter to letter.

Computer Keyboarding

Objective

Students will practice locating specific keys on a chalked computer keyboard.

What You Need

- sidewalk chalk
- computer key pattern on page 82
- computer keyboard diagram on page 82

Before You Begin

Discuss the importance of learning to keyboard without looking. Divide the class into three or four teams. Select a leader for each team. Using the patterns on page 82, have the team leaders draw large keyboards on the playground. Check the drawings for accuracy. Leave the keys blank. (You might want to label one or two letters on the home row to make sure students are in the correct position to start.)

What You Do

1. Send each team out to the playground and have students line up next to their team's keyboard outline.

2. When the teacher says "Go," have each team fill in the letters, numbers, and function keys on the keyboard as quickly as possible.

3. When a team has finished filling in all of the keys, its members shout "Enter." All students must stop and put their chalk down.

4. The teacher (or an appointed class member) checks the team's keyboard for accuracy. If any errors were made, the teacher notes them, but does NOT point them out to the team. The play continues.

5. The first team to correctly identify all of the keys wins.

Computer Keyboarding

Things to Think About

What memory devices can you use to remember where keys are located on the keyboard?

What letters or numbers are the easiest to remember?

Why is it important to know the position of the keys? Why can't you just look at what your fingers are doing?

How fast is a proficient typist? How fast can you keyboard?

Challenges

Have students research and reproduce the format of different keyboards. Why do they differ? Which ones do they prefer and why?

Have the students memorize the keys on an expanded keyboard. Include the numeric keypad, the arrow keys, and other position keys. Discuss the purpose of keys such as "num lock," "pg dn," or "ins."

More Ways to Play

Make up games using the computer keyboards and play them during recess or as extension activities.

Form two teams and have the team members "type" their spelling words. Students "type" the spelling word by hopping from letter to letter on the chalk drawings of the keyboards.

Computer Keyboarding

Computer Keyboard Patterns

Use heavy tagboard to make patterns for computer keys. Measure and cut 4 x 4", 4 x 6", and 4 x 8" rectangles. You may wish to round the corners.

Use the square pattern for letter keys "Q," "W," "R," etc. The medium-sized pattern is for keys such as "Enter" and "Caps Lock." Use the third pattern for long keys such as "Shift."

Trace around the patterns with chalk on blacktop or cement.

Note: Using this pattern will produce a keyboard approximately 5' x 1.5'

Multiplying in Grids

Objective

Students will practice the multiplication tables while filling them in on a grid. Make the drills more fun by working in relay teams.

What You Need

- sidewalk chalk
- two to four grids drawn on the playground (number of grids is dependent on size of class).
- one pair of large custom-made dice for each grid

Before You Begin

Draw the necessary number of grids on the playground (see page 85). Make a pair of dice for each grid (see page 14 for instructions on making dice). Mark one die with the numbers 4 through 9 and the other die with the numbers 2 through 7.

What You Do

1. Divide the class into two, three, or four teams.

2. Have each team line up in front of one of the grids that has been previously drawn.

3. The first player on each team rolls the dice, figures out the product of the two numbers (for example, 5 x 7 = 35), and writes the answer in the blank space where the two numbers intersect. Sometimes there is more than one possible square for a given answer. For example, the first student to roll a five and a seven would have a choice of two squares on the grid in which to write his or her answer. The next player to roll a five and a seven would automatically use the other square.

4. If the player's answer is incorrect, she loses her turn. Also, if a space has already been filled and there are no other choices available, the player loses her turn.

Multiplying in Grids

5. The first team to fill in its grid yells, "Facts filled!"

6. All teams gather around the finished grid. Any team can challenge the answers written in the grid. If any mistakes are found, that team is out and the game continues. The first team to fill in the grid correctly wins.

Things to Think About

What games can you play at home to help master the facts?

Is speed more important than accuracy when playing this game?

Challenges

Pretest your students to determine which math facts they most need to work on. Change the numbers on the dice to match those groupings. For example, one group might be working with standard dice with the numbers 1 to 6 and another group might be working with dice numbered 7 through 12.

Pair a student who knows his or her facts with a student who is having trouble in this area. Offer incentive points to the students who are willing to tutor others. The greatest challenge comes in taking on the responsibility of teaching another student.

Multiplying in Grids

	4	5	6	7	8	9
2						
3						
4				28		
5						
6						
7						

Graphing Ordered Pairs

Objective
Students will practice graphing ordered pairs on a large chalked grid using positive and negative numbers.

What You Need

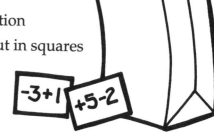

- sidewalk chalk
- two different colors of name tags for team identification
- one hundred 3 x 5 file cards or construction paper cut in squares
- felt marking pen
- bag

Before You Begin
Review the process of graphing ordered pairs. Remind students that the horizontal axis is always read first. For example, (+3, −1) would be at the intersection of +3 horizontal and −1 vertical. Practice graphing on the blackboard, on an overhead projector, or on graph paper.

Have one or two students chalk a large grid on the playground using the example on page 88. Have the rest of the class make a set of ordered pairs using the list on page 89 and the file cards. Place all the cards in a paper bag.

What You Do

1. Divide the class into two teams. Identify the team members by colored tags.

2. Place the bag of cards on the grid at point 0.

3. Have the first student walk to the center of the grid and draw a card from the bag and read it aloud. Moving on the grid line, the student goes to the point where he believes the pair intersects.

Graphing Ordered Pairs

4. His or her team must approve the location. A team can make one change without a penalty.

5. If the team's guess is still incorrect, the player must step off of the grid and it is the other team's turn. When a correct guess is made, the player remains standing at that intersection. A player from the other team goes to point 0 and draws a card.

6. After every student has had a turn, the team that has the most players in any one quadrant (A, B, C, or D) is declared the winner.

Things to Think About

Is there a reason why more students turned up in a particular quadrant?

How much does chance play in this game? How much does skill?

What is the one rule that you must remember when ordering pairs on a grid? (Horizontal axis first.)

Challenge

Have each student make a picture on a graph using connected dots to shape the picture. Have them to write down the ordered pairs for each dot. Ask students to trade lists of ordered pairs and see if a classmate can reproduce the pictures on a blank grid. Students can use the grid on page 90 or make one of their own.

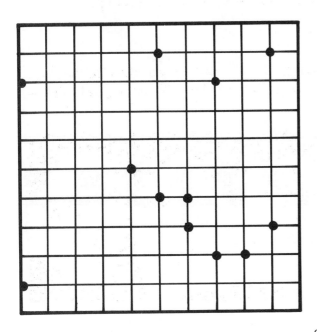 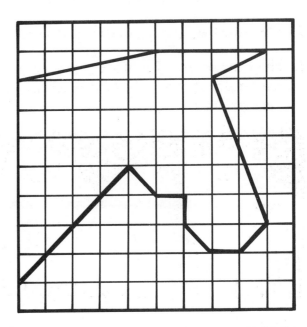

Graphing Ordered Pairs

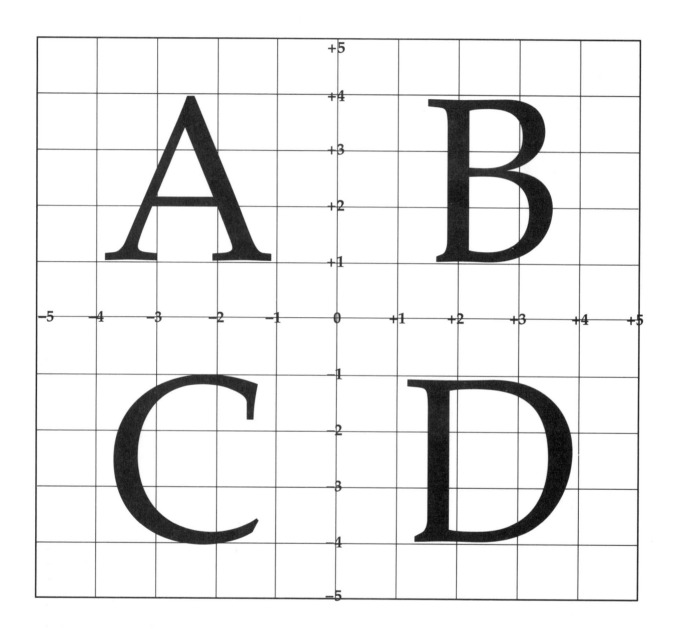

Graphing Ordered Pairs

Ordered Pairs List:

Write each of the ordered pairs on a file card. Place all of the file cards in a brown bag.

Left	−5 col	−4 col	−3 col	−2 col	−1 col	Right
+5,-5	−5, +1	−4, +1	−3, +1	−2, +1	−1, +1	+1,+5
+4,+5	−5, −1	−4, −1	−3, −1	−2, −1	−1, −1	+4,-5
+3,-4	−5, +2	−4, +2	−3, +2	−2, +2	−1, +2	+5,+5
+2,+4	−5, −2	−4, −2	−3, −2	−2, −2	−1, −2	−2,+1
+1,-3	−5, +3	−4, +3	−3, +3	−2, +3	−1, +3	+1,-4
−4,+1	−5, −3	−4, −3	−3, −3	−2, −3	−1, −3	−3,-1
−3,-1	−5, +4	−4, +4	−3, +4	−2, +4	−1, +4	+5,-4
−2,+2	−5, −4	−4, −4	−3, −4	−2, −4	−1, −4	−2,-2
−1,-2	−5, +5	−4, +5	−3, +5	−2, +5	−1, +5	+1,+4
+1,-5	−5, −5	−4, −5	−3, −5	−2, −5	−1, −5	+4,-4
+4,-2	+5, +1	+4, +1	+3, +1	+2, +1	+1, +1	−2,+3
+2+1	+5, −1	+4, −1	+3, −1	+2, −1	+1, −1	−3,+2
−2,-5	+5, +2	+4, +2	+3, +2	+2, +2	+1, +2	+5,-3
+1,+3	+5, −2	+4, −2	+3, −2	+2, −2	+1, −1	−2,-3
+4,+3	+5, +3	+4, +3	+3, +3	+2, +3	+1, +3	+4,+4
−2,+5	+5, −3	+4, −3	+3, −3	+2, −3	+1, −3	−3,-2
	+5, +4	+4, +4	+3, +4	+2, +4,	+1, +4	
	+5, −4	+4, −4	+3, −4	+2, −4	+1, −4	
	+5, +5	+4, +5	+3, +5	+2, +5,	+1, +5	
	+5, −5	+4, −5	+3, −5	+2, −5	+1, −5	

Bottom row: +1,-1 | +5,-1 | −3,+4 | −2,-4 | +1,+2 | +5,-2 | +4,-3 | −3,-3 | −2,+4

Graphing Ordered Pairs

Coordinate Grids For Geometric Figures

Start with two copies of this grid. Draw a picture on the first copy of the grid by marking dots at the intersection points and drawing lines to connect the dots. Write down the coordinates for each dot on a second copy of the grid and give it to your partner. Can your partner duplicate your drawing using just the ordered pairs? Can you duplicate your partner's drawing?

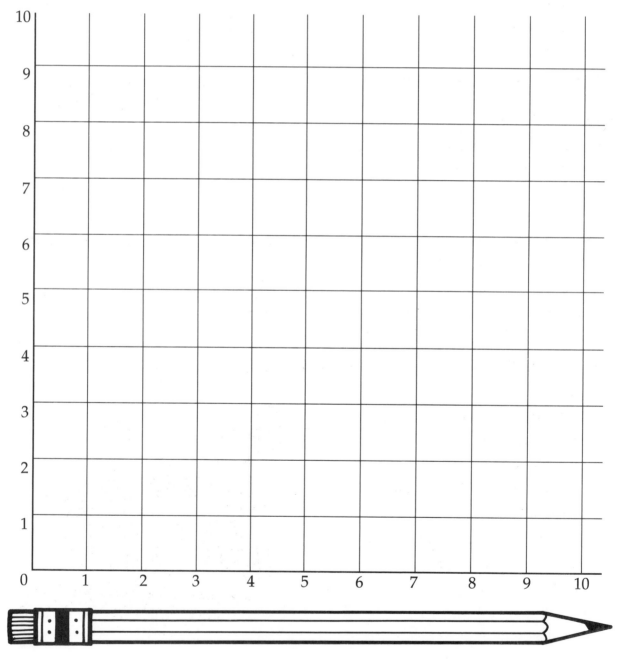

Chalking Geometric Terms

Objective

Students will practice geometric terminology by illustrating various shapes, angles, lines, and objects.

What You Need

- sidewalk chalk
- one ruler per student
- protractor
- teacher-prepared list of shapes to draw

Before You Begin

Review geometric terminology using the information on pages 93–94. Practice measuring a few angles with a protractor.

What You Do

1. Put students in groups of two or three and head for the playground. Find an area on the blacktop for the groups to work.

2. Read the directions and ask a student from each group to draw the geometric figure described. Students within a group may confer with each other, but should take turns drawing. Sample figures might include:

    - two parallel lines, one 5 inches in length and one 7 inches long
    - an isosceles triangle
    - two shapes that are symmetrical
    - two shapes that are congruent
    - a circle with a two-inch radius
    - a circle with a six-inch diameter
    - a triangle with an obtuse angle
    - a triangle with an acute angle
    - two lines that are equal in length

    (For additional ideas, refer to page 93–94.)

Chalking Geometric Terms

3. At the end of the lesson, one member from each team gets an answer sheet. The group members go over their work and correct any mistakes in their figures.

Things to Think About

Which geometric figures were the hardest to remember? What word associations can you think of to help remember the shapes or angles? (An *acute* angle is a small angle, a "cute" angle.)

Challenge

Ask students to write the definition for each geometric figure drawn. They can use chalk to write the definition underneath each figure.

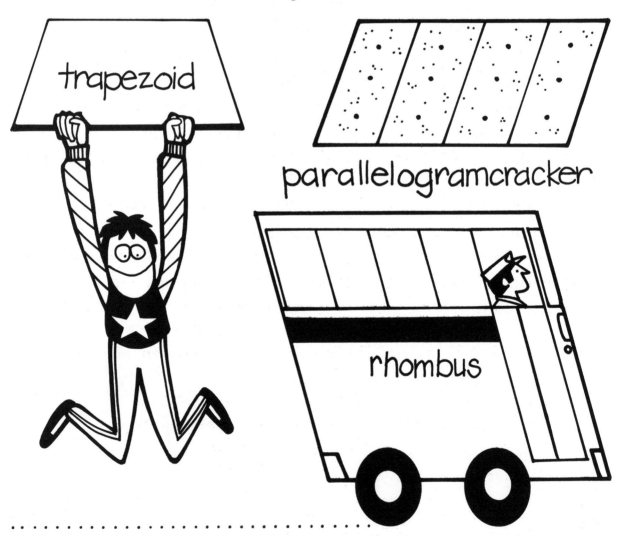

Chalking Geometric Terms

List of Geometric Terms and Shapes

acute angle	any angle that measures less than 90 degrees
acute triangle	a triangle with all angles less than 90 degrees
adjacent angles	angles that have a common vertex and a common side between them
circumference	the distance around a circle
complementary angles	two angles whose sum is 90 degrees (one right angle); each angle is called the complement of the other
congruent figures	shapes that coincide, or fit, on one another
diameter	a straight line drawn from any point of the outer rim of a circle, through the center, to the opposite side of the circle
equilateral triangle	a triangle with three equal sides
geometric figure	a point, line, plane, solid, or combination of these
hexagon	a regular six-sided figure
horizontal line	a straight line that goes straight across from left to right
isosceles triangle	a triangle with two equal sides
obtuse angle	any angle that measures more than 90 degrees, but less than 180 degrees
obtuse triangle	a triangle with one angle greater than 90 degrees
parallel lines	two lines that are equally distant from one another at all points
parallelogram	a quadrilateral where both pairs of opposite sides are parallel
perpendicular lines	two lines that form right angles when they intersect
polygon	a plane geometric figure bounded by three or more line segments that join without crossing one another
radius	a line drawn from the center of a circle to any point on the outer rim of the circle.
rectangle	a parallelogram with four right angles
rhombus	a parallelogram with two adjacent sides of equal length
right angle	an angle that measures 90 degrees
scalene triangle	a triangle with no equal sides

Chalking Geometric Terms

square   a parallelogram with four right angles and four sides of equal length

straight angle   an angle that measures 180 degrees; two sides lie on the same line

trapezoid   a quadrilateral having one pair of parallel sides

triangle   a three-sided figure, the sides of which are straight lines

vertex   a point where two lines meet

Drawings of Geometric Angles and Shapes

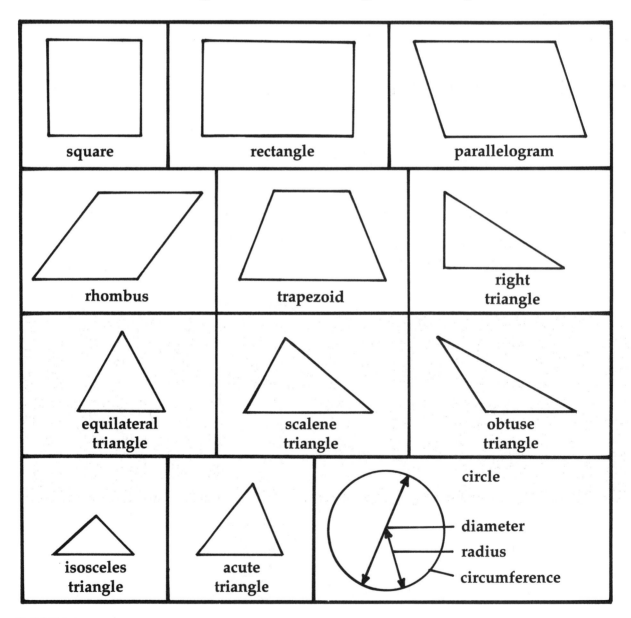

Finding Angles

Objective

Students will use the letters of the alphabet to identify and work with angles.

What You Need

- sidewalk chalk
- handouts of the alphabet in block letters with questions (see page 97)
- protractors (challenge work)

Before You Begin

Review with the class the various kinds of angles (acute, obtuse, straight, right, etc.) Refer to the list of geometric terms on pages 93–94.

Make sure the class understands how to form block letters. Practice writing block letters.

What You Do

Pass out chalk and the handouts of page 97 and head for the playground. Find a flat area where students can work.

Have each student use a copy of page 97 to draw the alphabet in large, block, capital letters.

Have students write the letters that answer the questions listed on page 97. (Teachers can use this list or make up their own.)

Finding Angles

Things to Think About

Is it hard to see angles in letters?

Look around you and find other objects that have angles, both indoors and outside.

What professions would need to have a good understanding of angles?

Challenges

Use a protractor to measure the angles in the letters you have drawn. Total the angles. Which letter has the highest sum?

Ask students to make a list at home of household objects that have angles (see page 98). Have them include objects with right angles, obtuse angles, and acute angles. They should identify each type of angle as they record it. See who can create the longest list.

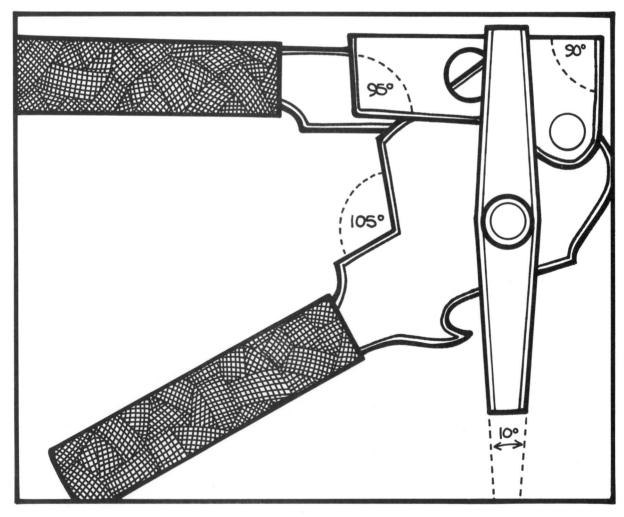

Finding Angles

Checking Alphabet Angles

Draw the alphabet on the playground using block letters, like the ones below.

A B C D E F G H I J K L M
N O P Q R S T U V W X Y Z

Answer the following questions:

1. Which letters have right angles?

2. Which letters have acute angles?

3. Which letters have acute *and* obtuse angles?

4. Which letter is a straight angle?

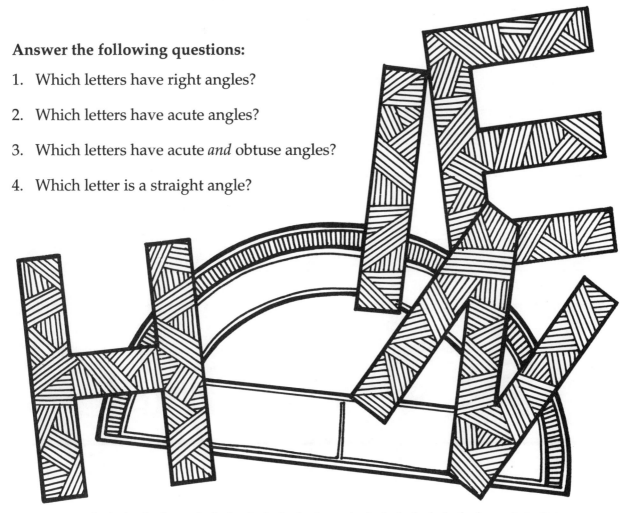

Answers: 1. B, D, E, F, H, L, P, R, T; **2.** A, K, M, N, V, W, X, Z; **3.** A, M, W, X, Y; **4.** I

Finding Angles

Hunting Angles at Home

Locate household objects that have right, obtuse, and acute angles. Identify one angle of each object, and record it on the lines below. If possible, measure each angle with a protractor and record your findings in the third column. Challenge: Try to complete the chart by finding four examples of each type of angle. The first one has been done for you.

Object	Type of Angle	Degrees
toaster	right	90°
	right	
	right	
	right	
	obtuse	
	obtuse	
	obtuse	
	obtuse	
	acute	
	acute	
	acute	
	acute	

Create a Monster

Objective

Students will practice various geometric exercises by designing and measuring line-segment monsters.

What You Need

- sidewalk chalk
- rulers and/or yardsticks (with both inches and centimeters given)
- a protractor for each group
- a calculator for each group

Before You Begin

Define the word *perimeter*. Discuss with the class the process of finding the perimeter of a figure (measuring the entire distance around it). Remind students that they can measure the perimeter of any shape with a ruler or yardstick as long as it is drawn with straight line segments only.

What You Do

1. Divide the class into groups of three to four students. (Students can also work on an individual basis.)

2. Find a working area on the playground.

3. Tell each group to design a monster using straight line segments only. Stress that the finished product should be large enough to measure easily, but small enough to be manageable.

Create a Monster

4. When the group has finished the monster, measure each line segment in inches. Add all the segments together. The total is the perimeter of the monster in inches. Record the answer on a piece of scratch paper.

5. Repeat the measuring process using centimeters.

6. Pair off with another group and try to estimate the perimeter of each other's monsters without using rulers.

Things to Think About

Is the size of the number larger when recorded in inches or centimeters?

Was it easier to guess the perimeter in inches or centimeters? Why?

Is it hard to draw a monster when you are restricted to straight line segments?

Challenges

Using a protractor, students can measure all of the angles in the monster to determine the total number of acute, obtuse, and right angles. (See pages 93–94 for definitions of various angles.)

Give each group a specific perimeter and see if group members can design a monster to fit that perimeter. The monster must be composed of at least 20 line segments.

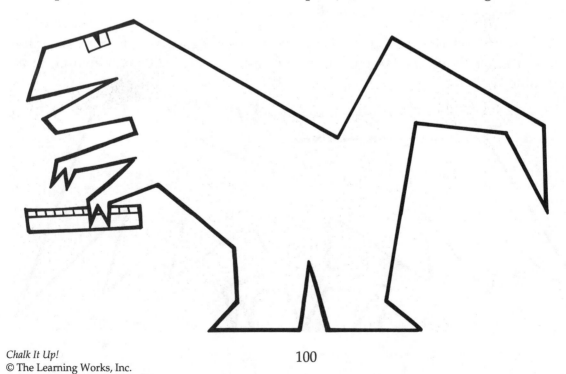

New Angles in Art

Objective

Students will start with a simple design and create a picture from it.

What You Need

- sidewalk chalk (white plus one color)

Before You Begin

Discuss various shapes and designs with the class. Look at completed pictures by artists. Try to find as many hidden geometric shapes as possible.

Draw a simple shape on the blackboard. Ask the class to brainstorm pictures that students could create using that basic shape. For example, a triangle could be the eye of a cat, the hat of a clown, or the sail on a boat.

What You Do

1. Pass out chalk and head for the playground. Have the students stand in a large circle. Ask them to stretch out their arms so that each student has enough space to draw on the blacktop or cement.

2. Ask each student to use a piece of colored chalk to draw a simple shape or design on the ground (curved line, half circle, L-shaped line, triangle, oval, etc.).

New Angles in Art

3. When the students are done, they should all rotate clockwise three positions. Each student should now be standing in front of a shape drawn by a classmate.

4. Using the white chalk only, the students should draw pictures, being sure to include the colored shape left by their classmate within the final design. Leave the pictures for other classes to enjoy.

Things to Think About

Discuss the fact that art may contain straight and/or curved lines.

Use the terms "realism" and "surrealism." Explain to the class that not all art reflects the way things appear in the real world.

Poll the class to determine personal preferences in art.

Challenges

Have each class member research a well-known artist to determine what style of painting he or she utilized (cubism, impressionism, etc.).

Ask students to draw a picture using straight lines only. See how many times they can incorporate the same shape in one drawing (as in the example below).

Shape:

Billboard Designs

Objective

Students will put together a billboard advertising a desirable personality trait.

What You Need

• sidewalk chalk

• billboard sketched on scratch paper

Before You Begin

Brainstorm with the class a lengthy list of desirable qualities (loyalty, kindness, caring) and undesirable personality traits (greediness, meanness, dishonesty).

Discuss the properties that make up an effective billboard (catchy phrasing, a few well-chosen descriptive words, easy-to-read typeface, and so forth).

What You Do

1. Have each student select one trait that he or she considers important in a friendship, such as honesty or a sense of humor.

2. On scratch paper, have each student put together a billboard advertising the trait that he or she has selected. Students can use a cliche such as "Curiosity Killed the Cat," or try something original:

Billboard Designs

3. Pass out chalk and assign an area of the playground for each student to work in. (For this activity, it might be fun to assign spots along a fence, around the perimeter of the playground, or in a large circle.)

4. Have each student chalk in his or her billboard, or the slogan from the billboard. Have the class walk around the area, sharing the billboards and slogans.

Things to Think About

Which parts of speech are especially important when creating a billboard (action words, descriptive words)?

Why is it usually best to avoid using too many words?

Which billboards or slogans have captured your attention and why?

Challenges

As a class, research how large the average billboard is and try to draw a billboard that size. Discuss the problems you encounter when you try to draw on such a large scale.

As a class project, create a "Burma Shave" style of advertisement along the edge of the playground. (Burma Shave advertised along the side of the road using a series of signs spaced several yards apart, each with a short phrase that when read in order made up a catchy sales pitch.) Have the students run down the row of signs and read them. Discuss how this was once a popular style of advertising.

More Ways to Play

Have students research a famous person and find a quote from him or her that they find meaningful. Chalk these words of wisdom around the school yard.

Games Kids Play

Objective

Students will invent new games to be played on the blacktop with chalk. They will practice writing clear, concise directions for their games and then teach the rules to a group of students.

What You Need

- sidewalk chalk
- spiral notebook or notebook paper/clipboard
- pens
- game equipment such as balls, jump ropes, markers (as needed)

Before You Begin

As a class, play several games from "Chalk Games to Play" at the end of this book.

Discuss the importance of clear directions. What consequences should be included to ensure that players follow the rules? Should rules be changed as the game progresses?

What You Do

1. Make up a new game, either individually or in groups.

2. Determine the object of the game and consider the following questions:

    a. What is the fewest number of players who can play the game? Is there a maximum number?

    b. Is the game played individually or in teams? How many teams? How many players per team?

    c. Who goes first or who is "it"? Can new players rotate in?

    d. What equipment is needed to play the game (markers, balls, jump ropes, etc.)?

    e. What do the players do?

    f. What rules are necessary to make the game flow smoothly?

    g. What rule infractions might occur, and what penalties should be given?

    h. When is the game over?

    i. How is the winner determined?

Chalk It Up!
© The Learning Works, Inc.

Games Kids Play

3. Design a chalk grid for playing the game.

4. Record the game rules on a piece of paper.

5. Groups should test their games by using their written rules to play them. They should add or change the instructions as necessary if something was unclear or didn't work or if questions needed to be answered.

6. Demonstrate the game to the rest of the class.

7. Have a play day using just the games created by the class.

Things to Think About

How did games come to be invented?

What makes a game popular? Why have some games been played for centuries while the popularity of others has waned?

What are some of the favorite games of class members?

Challenge

Design games that must be played without any other game pieces such as balls, markers, or dice.

More Ways to Play

Have the class design a game that can be played by all members of the class at the same time.

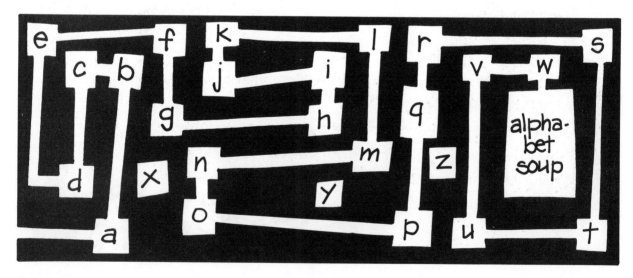

Buddy Play Day

Objective

Students will increase the communication bond between intermediate and primary students by creating games for the younger students to play.

What You Need

- sidewalk chalk
- game pieces (depending on rules of game)

Before You Begin

Pair the students in your classroom with students in a classroom at least three grades lower (i.e., first graders and fourth graders). The younger students are called "Little Buddies," and the older students are "Big Buddies."

What You Do

1. Divide your class into four or five groups.

2. Using the steps outlined in "Games Kids Play," pages 105–106, have each group design a game to be played by a group of Little Buddies.

3. Take both classes out onto the playground and play each of the games. Have the groups of Little Buddies move from game to game.

4. Ask your students to talk with their Little Buddies and get input on the games. What did they like? How could the game be improved?

Buddy Play Day

Things to Think About

What games were the favorites with the Little Buddies?

Which things were too difficult for them to do? How would you change the games in the future?

Challenge

As a class project, rework the games to improve them. Write down the new rules to the games and make game sets, patterns, and storage boxes. Present the completed game sets to the Little Buddies' classroom.

More Ways to Play

Trace your Little Buddy's outline on the playground. Have the Little Buddy trace your outline. Fill in such features as eyes, nose, ears, mouth, and hair.

Use the examples in "Chalk Warm-Ups," pages 15–18, to come up with additional ways Big Buddies can work with Little Buddies. For example, your students can help their Little Buddies take practice spelling tests or draw symmetrical designs.

Make sidewalk chalk with your Little Buddies (see page 7).

Chalk Games to Play

Getting Started

Whether you're introducing a new game or one that has been a favorite with children for years, game playing can be more than just fun, invigorating, outdoor exercise. Games provide an opportunity for students to learn strategy and to work in cooperative groups. For example, in the game "Fish in a Basket," one group of students works together to try to catch (or encircle) the other team. In "Capture the Flag," one team uses strategy to decoy the opposing team away from its flag.

Some games help students learn to memorize, sort, and categorize. In "Stormy Seas," a pair of students tries to think up a type of fish that the Tiger Sharks won't call out. The Tiger Sharks, on the other hand, must work together to guess as many types of fish as possible.

Many of the games on the following pages can also be adapted for use by teachers using the Integrated Thematic Instruction (ITI) model for lesson planning. For example, instead of coming up with types of fish for "Stormy Seas," adapt the game to your theme and have the students come up with names of endangered species, countries, famous explorers, or any number of categories. Likewise, the squares in "Categories" can all be chosen to fit your theme.

After playing the games in this section, have students talk about how they used strategy to improve their chances of winning. What part did skill play? How much was due to luck? In team sports, does cooperation improve your team's chances of winning?

Ask the students to determine the optimum number of players for the different games. How many people made the game the most exciting? When do more people lessen the fun? Finally, have the class think up new rules to play the same games.

109

Chalk Games to Play

Before You Begin

1. Discuss safety with the students. For obvious reasons, all the games in this section require only limited running on the blacktop surfaces. In addition, none of the games selected involve pushing or intentionally hitting another player with a ball.

2. Establish basic rules before beginning any playground game. Some games have many variations; make sure every player agrees on the variations that will be used.

3. Test new games and adjust the distances of goals and sizes of playing fields to suit the age, ability, and number of students in the class.

4. When a game requires fewer players than your class size, divide students into groups and make more than one playing grid. That's the advantage of using chalk. You can "chalk it up" as many times as necessary. For tag games, increase the number of chasers in larger classes. In relays, increase the number of lines or teams.

5. Discuss the concepts of sportsmanship and fair play. Encourage the students to practice both during the games.

6. Review the rules of the game and determine if a referee or umpire is needed. Many games require an independent individual to call faults (stepping on the line, bouncing the ball twice, throwing out of bounds) or to toss up jump balls.

Who Goes First

Here are some popular methods to use when deciding which person or team goes first:

- Choose the V.I.P. of the week.
- Pick the student who turned in the most assignments on time during the last week.
- Toss a coin.
- Pick a number between one and a hundred.
- Draw straws.
- Cut a deck of cards.

Categories

Number of Players

2 to 6

What You Need

- sidewalk chalk
- a small rubber ball or tennis ball

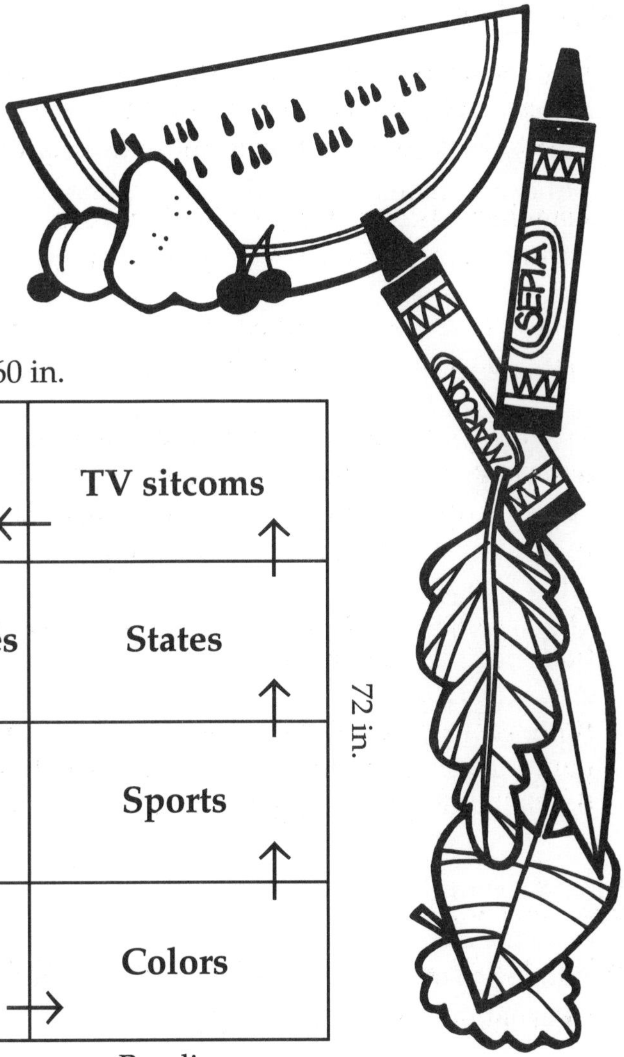

The Grid

60 in.

Fruits	TV sitcoms
Deciduous Trees	States
Holidays	Sports
Planets	Colors

72 in.

Baseline

Who Goes First

Each player should roll the ball to the end of the court. The player to get closest to the far end without going over, goes first, the next closest goes second, and so on.

How to Play

1. Each player thinks up his or her favorite category and writes it in a square. For example, one player might choose planets, another, rock stars. A good strategy for players is to choose a category they know a lot about but that the others might know little about.

2. The first player rolls the ball into the first category and runs to get it before it rolls out again. If he doesn't catch it in time, his turn is over.

111

Categories

3. If the player catches the ball before it rolls into another square, he bounces it once and shouts out an item in that category. For instance, if the first square is "states" and the second square "rivers," he would step into square one, bounce the ball once and say ALABAMA as he catches the ball. He would immediately step into the next square and without pausing, he would bounce the ball again, say RIO GRANDE or the name of another river as he catches the ball.

4. Players are not allowed to linger in any square while thinking of an answer.

5. A player may not repeat a name already used by another player. However, she can use her own selection again when going for doubles, triples, etc. For example: Sue calls out Alabama as her first state. On her second time through, she can call out ALABAMA, CALIFORNIA. On her third time, she can call out ALABAMA, CALIFORNIA, NEW YORK.

6. When a player steps on a line, fails to catch a bounce, or misses a category, his or her turn is over. On his or her next turn, he must start at the first square again.

7. If a player makes it all the way through the grid without a mistake, he or she rolls the ball into the second category and starts around the grid again. This time, however, he or she must name two items in each category.

More Ways to Play

Make all the categories fit one theme. For example if you were studying world geography, the categories might be countries, capital cities, continents, bodies of water, major rivers, land formations, and so forth.

Capture the Flag

Number of Players

20 to 40 divided into two equal teams

What You Need

- sidewalk chalk
- colored tags to identify the team players (see page 10 for instructions)
- two flags or handkerchiefs of different colors

The Grid

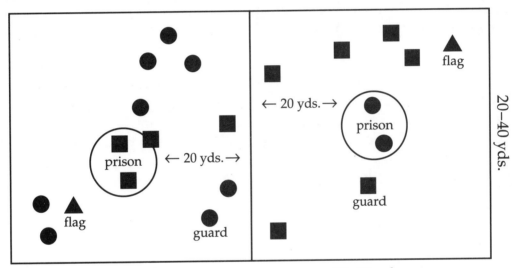

● = Team 1

■ = Team 2

▲ = Flag

Who Goes First

Agree upon a signal to start the game, such as blowing a whistle or ringing a bell.

113

Capture the Flag

How to Play

1. Set up the playing field as shown in the grid on page 113. Divide the class into equal teams identified by colored name tags. Give each group a flag.

2. Each team places its flag somewhere on its side of the field. The object of the game is to steal the other team's flag and carry it across the center line without being tagged.

3. Flags can be placed anywhere on a team's side of the playing field. Team members should use strategy to confuse the other team regarding the real location of the flag.

4. Any players tagged while in enemy territory are placed in prison. Each team should appoint one or two players to guard its prison. Guards should stand 15 to 20 feet away from the prison.

5. Prisoners must keep at least one foot in prison at all times until they are rescued. If a prisoner's teammate successfully eludes the guard(s) and touches the prisoner's hand without being tagged, the prisoner is freed. Both players receive free passage to their side of the field. A player can only rescue one prisoner at a time.

6. At the end of the play period, if neither team has successfully captured the other team's flag, the team with the most prisoners wins.

More Ways to Play

Have each team place more than one flag on its side of the field. The opposition must capture all of the flags.

What's the Time?

Number of Players

7 to 30

What You Need

- sidewalk chalk

The Grid

Draw a long line across the playground. On one side of the line, about 100 feet away, make a three-foot diameter circle to represent home base.

Who Goes First

Use your favorite method for selecting the first two Keepers of the Time or use one of the suggestions on page 110.

How to Play

1. The Keepers of the Time should secretly agree upon a time of day. (Limit choices to the hour and half hour.) They should also decide which one of them will be PM and which one AM.

2. The remainder of the students stand single file along the line.

3. The Keepers of the Time walk down the row of students. Each student tries to guess the time, specifying AM or PM as well.

115

What's the Time?

4. When a student guesses the correct time, the chase begins. For example, if the time is 10:00 AM, the PM Keeper of the Time would shout "Go," and the guesser would chase the AM Keeper to the clock tower. If the time were 10:00 PM, the AM Keeper would shout "Go," and the guesser would chase the PM Keeper.

5. If the guesser tags the Keeper of the Time before he or she reaches the clock tower, the guesser takes his or her place as a Keeper and the play starts over. The other Keeper does not change.

Other Rules

The Keepers of the Time must not walk or stand more than three feet from the line.

The guesser may not step over the line until a Keeper of the Time shouts "Go."

Stormy Seas

Number of Players

10 to 40

What You Need

- sidewalk chalk

The Grid

Draw two- to three-foot diameter circles, evenly scattered around the playing area. Draw one less circle than half the number of students. For instance, if you have 30 students, make 14 circles.

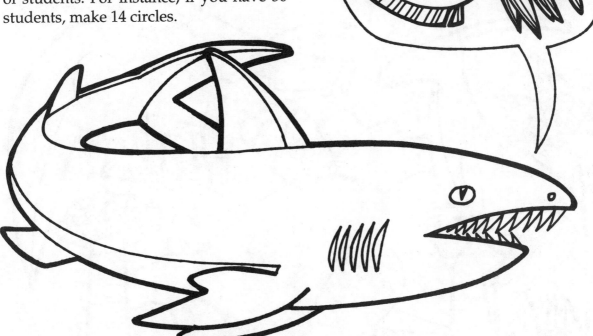

How to Play

1. Divide the class into pairs. Appoint one pair to be the Tiger Sharks. Each of the remaining pairs should stand in one of the circles.

2. Each pair secretly assumes the name of a type of fish (salmon, perch, bass, trout, goldfish, etc.).

3. The Tiger Sharks move around the circles calling out all the names of fish that they can think of. If a couple's fish is called, the two leave their circle and fall in behind the Tiger Sharks, following them around the field.

Stormy Seas

4. When the Tiger Sharks can't think of any more types of fish, they shout "Stormy Seas." All the pairs who are no longer in the safety of a circle, including the Tiger Sharks, run for an empty circle.

5. The pair left without a circle becomes the new Tiger Sharks for the next game.

More Ways to Play

Playing this game is a wonderful way of teaching children to memorize any number of things. Instead of using fish, have the students choose types of whales, endangered wildlife, planets and other astrological bodies (sun, moon, comets, constellations), dinosaurs, colors, or geometrical shapes.

Crazy Canvas

Number of Players

5 to 10

What You Need

- sidewalk chalk

The Grid

Mark an "X" where the Painter is to begin drawing. The remainder of the grid is drawn as the game proceeds.

Who Goes First

Choose your favorite method of determining the player order.

How to Play

1. One player is chosen to be the Painter and stands at the X. Using a piece of chalk, she begins drawing a twisting line as she walks backwards away from the X.

2. The rest of the players are Brushes. The first Brush counts to 10 and then starts following the line wherever it goes. Once the first Brush has left the starting point, the next Brush counts to 10 and then starts off.

Crazy Canvas

3. At any time, the Painter can turn the line and intersect with lines that have already been drawn. At the first intersection, she writes a 1. The first Brush must stop at that intersection and go to the starting X.

4. The other Brushes may proceed through intersection 1. As they start to gain on the Painter, she turns the line again and intersects with another line and writes 2. The second Brush must stop at intersection 2 and go back to the starting X.

5. The play continues. Each time the Brushes start to gain on the Painter, she intersects a line and writes down the number of the next Brush. That Brush must stop at the intersection and go back to the starting X. However, the Brushes only have to stop at an intersection one time. The next time they come to that intersection, they can proceed through it without stopping.

6. If any of the players catch the Painter, the Painter is out and a new game begins.

7. If the Painter is able to reconnect her line to the starting X without being caught, the play reverses. The Painter now chases the brushes. If a Brush makes it back to his intersection point without being tagged, he jumps off the "canvas" to safety.

8. If a Brush is tagged by the Painter, he becomes the next Painter. If all the Brushes make it to safety without being tagged, select a new Painter for the next game.

Fox and Geese

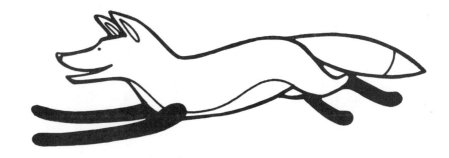

Number of Players

10 to 15

What You Need

- sidewalk chalk

The Grid

Draw a large circle 30 feet in diameter and divide it into six sections.

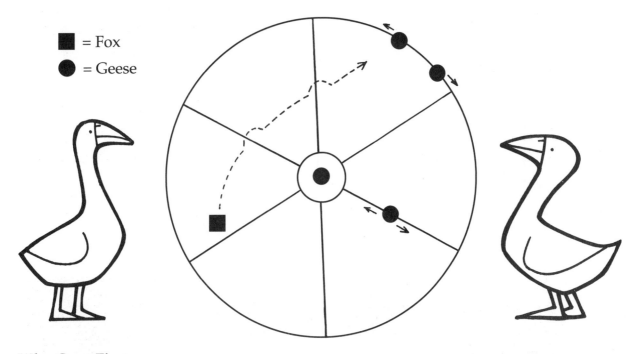

■ = Fox

● = Geese

Who Goes First

Select a player to be the Fox by using your favorite method or one of the suggestions on page 110.

How to Play

1. Assign one player to be the Fox. The remaining players are geese and should stand on the line that forms the wheel's hub. If a goose is tagged by the Fox, she is out of the game.

2. Geese may run in any direction along the hub or along the spokes of the grid. However, they must be on a line at all times. The Fox can only run in the open spaces and may jump across the spokes.

Fox and Geese

3. A goose can rest in the center circle for as long as he or she likes. However, only one goose can be in the circle at a time. If a second goose enters, the first goose must leave.

4. The game is over when the Fox has tagged all of the geese. A new Fox is chosen and the games starts again.

More Ways to Play

Try drawing different shapes and connecting them together to form a grid.

Keep Away

Number of Players

5 to 15

What You Need

- sidewalk chalk
- playground ball

The Grid

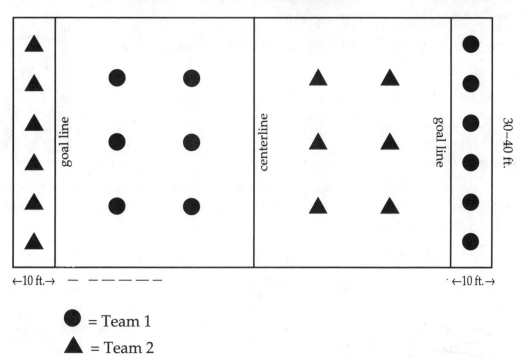

● = Team 1

▲ = Team 2

How to Play

1. Divide the class into two equal groups. Each group should position half its players as Fielders in the playing area and the other half as Ends on the opposite side of the field.

2. Toss the ball into the air in middle of the court. The Fielders try to catch the ball and throw it across to their Ends. The Fielders on the opposite side try to intercept the ball and throw it back across the center line to their own Ends.

3. If the ball goes out of bounds, the Fielder nearest the ball retrieves it and throws it back into play.

Keep Away

4. Each time the ball is successfully caught in the end zone, a point is scored. The team with the most points at the end of the playing period wins.

5. You may wish to divide the playing period into five-minute quarters and rotate Ends and Fielders at each quarter.

Other Rules

Whenever a foul is made, the ball is given to the nearest Fielder on the opposing team. If members from both teams foul simultaneously, the ball is tossed between them like a jump ball in basketball. The following are fouls:

- moving out of bounds for any reason other than to retrieve a ball
- dribbling the ball
- carrying the ball
- holding the ball for more than five seconds

More Ways to Play

Position all players at least six feet apart. Do not allow the Ends to move more than one step in any direction to catch the ball. Do not allow the Fielders to move more than one step in any direction to intercept the ball.

Change the end zone to corner zones. Follow the same rules. (See the diagram below.)

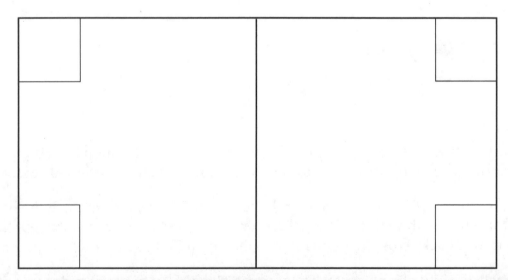

Red and Blue

Number of Players

20 to 40

What You Need

- sidewalk chalk
- a medium-sized cube with half the faces colored blue and the other half red. You can cover a classroom die with colored paper or make one using the instructions on page 14.

The Grid

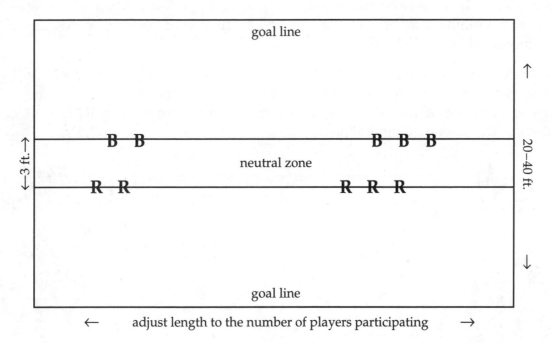

goal line

↑

3 ft.→

B B   B B B

neutral zone

R R   R R R

20–40 ft.

↓

goal line

←   adjust length to the number of players participating   →

How to Play

1. Divide the class into two teams: red and blue (or any two colors or objects). Position each team on one side of the grid.

2. Have each team member sit with a hand, foot, or some portion of his or her body touching the neutral zone.

3. Toss the cube into the neutral zone. If a blue surface lands face up, the blue team members run for their goal line, and the red team chases them.

Red and Blue

4. If the red team catches any blue team members before they cross the line, the tagged players become red team members.

5. One player may tag as many players as he or she wants. A tagged player cannot become a tagger until the next play.

6. When the play period ends, the team with the most players on its side wins.

More Ways to Play

Tagged players become prisoners of the opposite team and stand behind the goal line. Instead of becoming members of the opposition, they shout advice or counsel to the remaining members of their own team.

Divide the class into four teams and use the grid shown below. Use two dice, each with four colors marked at random. When the dice are rolled, the members of the teams whose colors are up run for their goal lines. All of the other teams try to tag them. Tagged players become members of the team that tagged them.

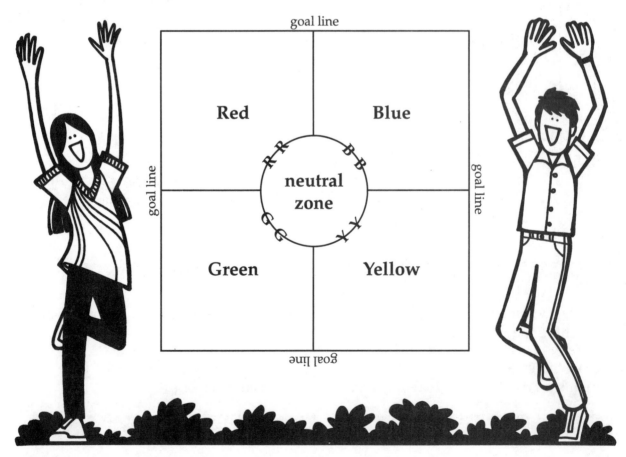

Four Square

Number of Players

Four players at a time; any number can rotate in

What You Need

- sidewalk chalk
- medium-sized (10-inch) playground ball

The Grid

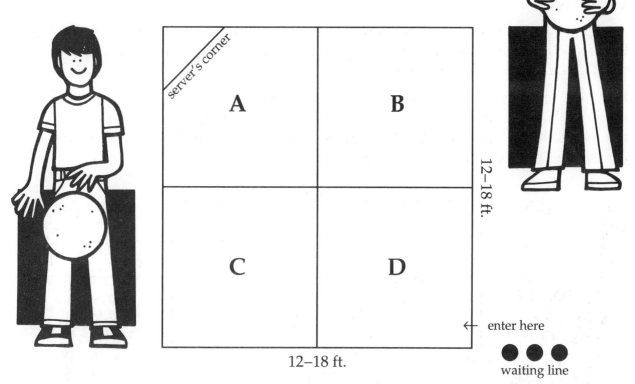

server's corner

A   B

C   D

12–18 ft.

12–18 ft.

← enter here

waiting line

Who Goes First

The class may choose its own method for determining who goes first or use one of the suggestions on page 110.

How to Play

1. The server and three other players each stand in one of the four squares on the grid. The server stands in the server's square.

2. The server bounces the ball once in his square and then hits the ball into one of the other three squares by batting it underhanded, either with an open hand or his fist.

127

Four Square

3. The player receiving the ball lets it bounce once in her square before batting it to another player.

4. Volleying continues back and forth between the squares until a player makes a mistake, or faults.

5. When a player faults, he must leave the diagram. The remaining players each move up one square. For example, if B faulted, C would move to B, D would move to C, and the next player in line would enter square D.

Other Rules

If a player commits any of the following mistakes, she must leave the court and go to the end of the line:

- volleying the ball before it bounces
- hitting the ball on a line
- hitting the ball overhand
- catching, holding, or carrying the ball on a return volley
- returning a ball after another player has faulted
- serving from anywhere other than the server's corner

- batting the ball out of bounds
- being hit by a ball

Roly-Poly

Number of Players

2 to 6

What You Need

- sidewalk chalk
- small rubber bouncing ball

The Grid

60 in.

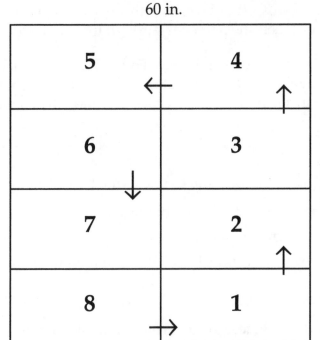

72 in.

baseline

Who Goes First

Select your own method or use one of the suggestions on page 110.

How to Play

1. The first player rolls the ball into the first square and then runs after it, retrieving it before it rolls out of the square.

2. Once she retrieves the ball, she bounces it once in square one. Then she steps into square two and bounces the ball again.

Roly-Poly

3. She continues bouncing the ball in each square until she finishes the diagram. This is referred to as "Ones."

4. When the player has finished her Ones, she rolls the ball into square two, and again, runs to retrieve it before it rolls out.

5. She then bounces the ball and bats the rebound with the palm of her hand, catching the ball with both hands on the second rebound. She continues stepping through the squares, bouncing the ball twice in each square.

6. After completing her "Twos," the player rolls the ball into square three, recovers it, and bounces it three times. Then she proceeds through the diagram.

7. When the player has completed her Threes, Fours, Fives, and Sixes, she must "prove herself." To prove herself, the player steps through the diagram, bouncing the ball once in square one, twice in square two, three times in square three, and so on.

Other Rules

A player loses her turn whenever she makes one of the following mistakes:

*   fails to retrieve the ball before it rolls out of the square
*   bounces the ball the incorrect number of times
*   catches the ball between bounces instead of batting it on the rebound

More Ways to Play

To make the game more difficult, set a ground rule of not catching the ball between squares or add one of the following tricks:

Swing your right or your left leg over the ball as it bounces.

Clap your hands once or twice on each bounce.

Alternate hands when bouncing the ball, first with your right hand and then with your left hand.

Bounce the ball and then spin around and catch it.

Bounce the ball, jump in the air, make a full-body turn, and then catch the ball.

Hopscotch

Number of Players

2 to 4 players

What You Need

- sidewalk chalk
- one marker per player (see instructions on pages 12 and 13 for making markers from paper or use a key, beanbag, hair clip, or similar object)

The Grid

Basic Hopscotch is played on a grid composed of 10 compartments. Hopscotch grids can measure up to 5 feet at the base line and up to 15 feet in length. However, most students complain that such grids are too large: "No one ever steps on a line or misses a turn." A few popular grid styles are illustrated on page 134.

Who Goes First

To begin the game, each player stands at the baseline of the grid and tosses his marker to the far end. The player whose marker lands closest to compartment 10 goes first, the next closest goes second, and so forth.

How to Play

1. Stand at the baseline and throw your marker into the first compartment.

2. Hop over the first compartment and land on either one foot or two feet, depending on the layout of the grid. For example, if you are using grid A, land with one foot in compartment 2 and the other foot in compartment 3. If you were using grid B, you would land on one foot in compartment 2 and then hop on one foot into compartment 3 before landing on two feet in compartments 4 and 5.

131

Hopscotch

3. Continue hopping alternately on one foot and then two through the grid (skipping any compartments with markers in them) until you reach the last compartment.

4. Upon arriving at the last compartment (10), hop out of the grid, and then reversing direction, hop back through the grid. After landing in compartments 2 and 3, bend over, pick up your marker, hop into compartment 1 landing on one foot, and then hop out of the grid.

5. Next, toss your marker into the second compartment and repeat the process, this time hopping first in compartment 1 on one foot and then in compartment 3 on one foot, skipping over compartment 2, which contains your marker.

6. On each successive turn, throw your marker into the next compartment in numerical sequence.

7. All players who successfully complete the grid are winners.

Other Rules

Whenever you break a rule, leave your marker in the compartment you last successfully completed and go to the back of the line. You lose your turn if you make any of the following errors:

- stepping on a line or in a compartment that is occupied by another player's marker
- failing to throw the marker completely within the correct compartment
- touching the ground with your raised foot
- not hopping in the compartments in the proper sequence
- hopping more than once in one compartment

Hopscotch

More Ways to Play

To increase the difficulty of the game, have the students vary the size of the compartments within the grid itself; for example, have the compartments become larger or smaller as you progress from 1 to 10. You can also try one of the hopscotch versions below.

Kick-and-Hop Scotch

1. Toss your marker into compartment 1 and then hop into that compartment, landing on one foot. Without moving your stationary foot, kick the marker over the baseline using your other foot. Then, hop out of the compartment.

2. Toss your marker into the second compartment. Hop in compartment 1, and then compartment 2. Kick your marker out over the baseline and hop out.

3. Repeat the process, tossing your marker into each compartment in numerical sequence. (Note: You lose a turn if your marker fails to land within the correct compartment, you step on a line, hop out of sequence, hop more than once in one compartment, or fail to kick the marker across the baseline.)

Kick Scotch

1. Toss your marker into the first compartment, hop into the compartment and kick the marker into compartment 2.

2. Hop into compartment 2 and kick the marker into compartment 3.

3. Continue this process until you reach compartment 10. (Note: You lose your turn if you kick your marker too far or not far enough, or if the marker lands on a line.) Other fouls include those for regular hopscotch.

Territory

Play this version according to the rules of regular hopscotch with the following exception. When you have successfully completed one turn, stand with your back to the grid and toss your marker over your shoulder. The square your marker lands in belongs to you. The other players cannot land in that square.

Hopscotch

Sample Hopscotch Grids

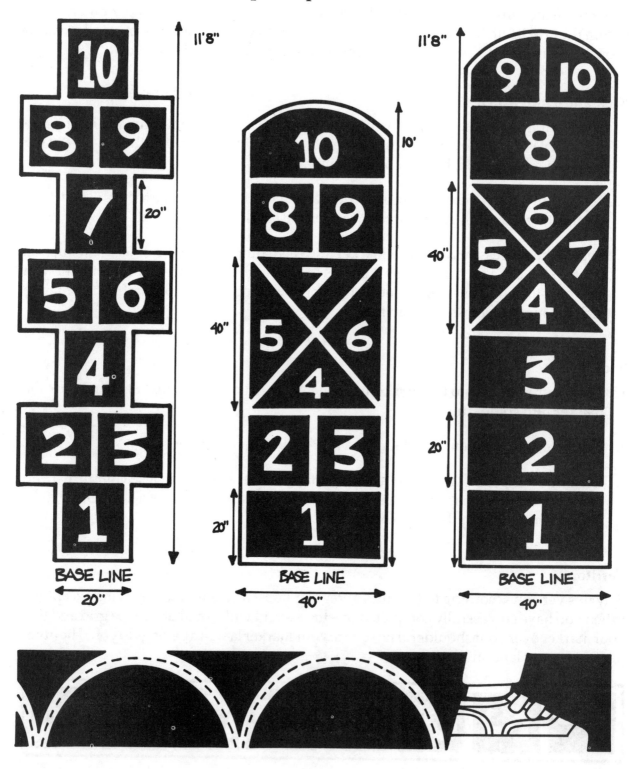

Fish in the Basket

Number of Players

8 to 12

What You Need

• sidewalk chalk

The Grid

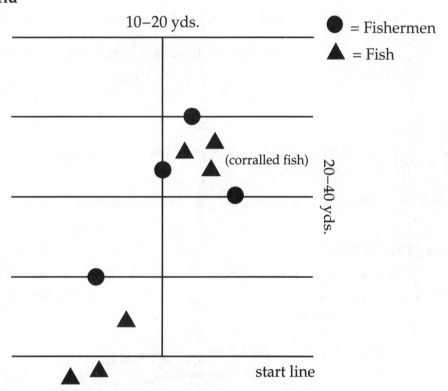

10–20 yds.

● = Fishermen

▲ = Fish

(corralled fish)

20–40 yds.

start line

How to Play

1. Select four students to be Fishermen. Three Fishermen should stand on the horizontal lines of the grid. The fourth stands on the centerline. Each Fisherman can only move on the line to which he is assigned. The remainder of the students are the Fish, and they may move anywhere on the court.

2. The Fish try to run from one end of the court and back again. Meanwhile, the Fishermen try to trap all of them in one square by surrounding them on three sides. Before the play begins, allow the students a few moments to plan their strategy. Note: The Fish are not allowed to "bully" their way out of the trap by physically overpowering a Fisherman. A Fish is considered "caught" if she can be tagged by a Fisherman when she tries to move in any direction.

135

Fish in the Basket

3. If a Fish makes it across the court and back again, he may call out "Ice." The Fishermen must freeze, and then all the fish may take one giant step in any direction. When all of the Fish have moved, a Fisherman calls out "Fire" and play continues.

4. Each Fish can only yell "Ice" once during the game. Students can use strategy to determine the best time to use it, for example, when only one Fish is left on the court, and taking a giant step would move her safely away from a Fisherman.

5. If a Fish is tagged by a Fisherman, he must go back to the start line and begin again.

6. The game is over when all of the Fish make it safely across the grid, or they are trapped in a square.

Other Rules

Fishermen cannot step off of their assigned lines. They may not move onto adjoining lines even at intersection points.

Fish may not leave the sides of the court to avoid getting caught.

More Ways to Play

In the Malayan version of this game (called Calah Panjang or Bamboo Long), there are six Fishermen—one on the start and finish lines as well. The Fishermen simply tag the Fish instead of corralling them.